INSIG

INSIGHTS

A Life Companion

Sandra Rajpaul

Sanguhla Impressions

Published by: Sanguhla Impressions
Cover layout and book format: Suzanne EL-Oud

The author of this book does not dispense any medical advice nor prescribe the use of any technique as a medical treatment without you obtaining advice from a medical practitioner. The intent of the author is only to offer information of a general nature to help you in your quest for mental, emotional, and spiritual well-being. In the event, you use any of the information in this book for yourself or others, the author assumes no responsibility for your actions.

If any events relayed in this book closely relate to your particular experience or story, it is purely coincidental.

Paperback ISBN: 978-0-9879825-2-0
eBook ISBN: 978-0-9879825-3-7

Dedication

In loving memory of my parents,
Ram Gahan and Molly Rajpaul,
and to my siblings,
Dinna Rajpaul-Bainey,
Rama Oliver (Tony) Rajpaul,
and Barry Rajpaul.

I appreciate and love you all dearly.

Contents

Note from Author

I honor you for your interest in this book. It says that your life matters, and how you live and experience it are invaluable and priceless to you. It also conveys that others are important to you as you impact their lives. As such, it is my sincere hope that this book becomes a family jewel and keepsake in your home. I commend you for taking this step to write an awesome story for your life as you embrace these insights, which I trust will become your life companion.

This book started as a small project a couple of years ago but eventually evolved into a set of insights based on life lessons as I paid attention to life and my state of being. Although these insights arose from looking in the mirror, I kept referring to them whenever I felt challenged in a particular area in my life. That is when I told one of my friends, Ron that I was going to present this book as a life companion, because everybody will be tried and tested, and would need wisdom on their side. The best friend to help you up is wisdom itself. I believe these insights will help you to gracefully navigate your way through what often seems like the insanity of life, as they promise to guide, transform, heal and restore.

May you have the courage to listen to your life's longings, and use the insights as a compass so that your life experience feels richer and fuller. I invite you to share with me your experience as you incorporate these insights into your life.

May you breathe easier, become more relaxed within, savor the preciousness of life, dance to the beat of your own drum, bravely explore what lies in your heart as you dare to be bold, cherish your relationships, grow and evolve, discover who you truly are, and much more. May you be blessed with peace, joy, a fullness within, and an amazing sense of freedom.

Warmly,

Sandra

www.sandrarajpaul.com

1.

Examine to What You Are Saying "Yes" and "No"

Every time, you say "No" to something you are also simultaneously saying "Yes" to something else, and vice versa. For example, when you say "No" to investing your time in engaging in something inspirational or taking some rest time, you are simultaneously saying "Yes" to inviting in stress. When you say "Yes" to taking committed, responsible and disciplined measures to prosper your life, you are also saying "No" to staying in a downtrodden situation.

Before you say "Yes" or "No" to something or someone, determine what it is you truly want, and say "Yes" to what benefits your life in a positive and progressive way. In other words, say "Yes" to what is really important and "No" to the unimportant that does not serve you well. Take some time out and pay close attention to what you have been saying "Yes" and "No." Now adjust accordingly.

As you go about your day, with each encounter remember that every time you are negative and condescending toward others including your spouse, children, family, friends, associates, and employees you are saying "Yes" to destroying your relationships, and "No" to creating a strong foundation. Likewise, whenever you are encouraging and supportive of these people in the right way, you are saying "Yes" to creating a healthy and solid relationship with those who matter, and "No" to a rocky and destructive relationship with them.

If you want to live a life full of hope, opportunities, and possibilities then say "Yes" to keeping company with vibrant, encouraging and expansive influences, and "No" to the small thinkers who limit you. Do not let anyone distract you with their ongoing negativity by saying "No" to them. In the process, you will be saying "Yes" to maintaining a positive outlook and a life of purpose and meaning.

You have it in you to make this day a fulfilling and joyous one by consciously determining what to say "Yes" and "No" to in the choices you make. So, go ahead and make smart choices today because you can.

2.

Write the Story of Your Life Hereon

It is time to take the pen away from everyone who has been writing the story of your life. Take it and start writing the story you truly want to live. Every moment presents a new opportunity to write the story of your life thereon; to start a new chapter. Your past does not define you so leave it behind where it belongs. All you need to bring into the present are the lessons learned from your past experiences that are useful for your transformation, and advancement.

As you write your story, remember that impossible is for non-believers. Believers are the ones who take practical steps in faith while staying open to receive inner-guidance and making the most of what shows up along the way. Even when things do not turn out the way you hope as you write your story, at least you know that you are holding the pen in your hand, and can take the story in a direction that you prefer. Each step you take will build your confidence. So, go ahead and take a step. Then take another and keep going.

This moment asks of you to step out in faith; be brave, and write the story that resonates with you according to your natural rhythm, and you will start to feel more at ease within as you find yourself in your zone where it feels right and natural to you. As you do so, mind your own business about you. Do not mind other people's business about you, that is, their opinions and criticisms that are meant to devalue and discourage you otherwise, you will be handing them back the pen.

Whatever story you decide to write always remember to become a better person in the process. Whichever direction you take, let the inner compass guide you to help others and improve the world because of who you are and in what you do to be a beautiful part of your story. So, hold your pen confidently and steadily. Be creative and write a fresh, new and awesome story for your life!

3.

Know Your Purpose

If you believe you have a great purpose to serve on this earth, you will not be wondering what it is. You will know it. You would not have to go through some exercise to help you determine what that purpose is. Often, the problem in finding one's purpose is that people tend to feel it is supposed to be something spectacular and comparable to what someone whom they admire is doing and that it should bring them a lot of money and attention. As such, they are allowing this concept to cloud their view and hence, clarity to know their purpose.

If you believe you have some purpose to serve other than what is before you right now, you would know it when you let go inwardly of everyone and everything that shroud it. You would go beyond your fears of leaving behind what is familiar, as fears hinder not help. You would let go of all your preconceived notion about the false purpose that it is supposed to serve, such as being impressive to others.

Only then your purpose would have a greater meaning and purpose, as it would emerge from a deeper space within you that is true to you, whereby you do not lose your soul even if it brings you a lot of money and recognition.

In trying to find your purpose, sometimes it finds you, or you are led to it, or accidentally come upon it. At other times, you just know it as it pulls at you and does not leave you alone. Often, this is something that you did naturally from childhood. When you cannot figure out what it is, let it go and in the meantime continue to do something, as through this you and your purpose can eventually meet up. In finding your purpose, it is not necessarily about pursuing your passion as a livelihood, nor is it exclusive of it. It, however, entails using your gifts and talents passionately, energetically and usefully during the life of the purpose.

The physical expression of that purpose is there for you to fulfill an unfulfilled desire, but most importantly it is there so that you could learn something about yourself through it. As such, your purpose may express itself in different ways at different stages in life as you change.

How you attain, use, and evolve consciously through your purpose is the secret behind it, and the real reason for it. The physical expression of your purpose is merely an instrument or a platform for your evolution, not a goal. The goal is your evolution through it. So go ahead, explore yourself, find your purpose, be at peace with what you discover, and use it well.

4.

Build a Worthy Opinion of Yourself

It is quite common for people to place too much credence in other people's opinions of them and what they do to the extent that they wreak havoc in one's life. As such, this sucks your energy and life-force, which affects your ability to function optimally. In which case, you are using other people's negative opinions of you to become your excuse to stay down, be held back, and debilitated.

Instead of giving people power over your life by bringing you down with their negative opinions, determine if there is any substance in what they are saying. It is the best attitude to adopt as it would benefit you. To do so, you must not get emotionally involved and lost in what is said. Become the objective observer as it will allow you to rationalize if there is any worth in their comments. If there is, use it to your advantage to fix what is needed in you, as this is for your well-being. If there is no value then prove them wrong by proving yourself right about you, and what you can do.

It is wise not to have the unrealistic expectation of others to believe in you unless you first believe in yourself and in a higher power. Make the opinion of yourself a solid and beautiful one built on a strong and stable foundation, but with room for improvement. Then other people's opinions of you will not be able to shake you, nor break you down as you are open, flexible and ready to transform if needed. In this way, you have claimed authority over your life instead of giving it over to others.

Life is such that you will meet people along the way who are envious of you and not want to see you progress and succeed. Their opinions will even come disguised and appear as well-intended comments from sources, such as family, friends, associates, followers, competitors, strangers, influential people and authoritative figures.

Do not give unwarranted attention to these people and what they say. Think well of yourself and let that have power over their opinions. Now you can proceed to unleash your potential and forge ahead confidently knowing that you are energetically co-operating fully with a higher power that directs your life. Relax and enjoy the journey.

5.

Choose Your Words Wisely

Every spoken word has power in it as it is energetic, and vibrates at a frequency that materializes accordingly. Spoken words that are negative and defeating vibrate at a gross level to keep you and others down, and push good people away. Spoken words that are positive and encouraging are light. They vibrate at a high frequency that uplifts you and others and draws inspiring people in, and those who seek to become productive and evolved human beings.

Every word spoken touches not only the receiver but also you. As such, it is imperative to become deliberately aware of your choice of words which are in direct alignment with your pattern of thinking, and external expression. Negative words come from your association with negative thoughts that can affect and hurt not only others but also definitely hurt you, as they dilute the good in you and what you do. Likewise, positive words come from your connection with positive thoughts and inspirational influences, which defeat negativity to bring out good.

Start noticing your choice of words and tone of voice as you speak and express yourself. Do your language and tone of voice speak a winner or a victim, a believer or a doubter, a positive or negative person, an inspiring or hopeless being, an agitated spirit or someone who speaks their truth with quiet confidence, a sensitive or self-absorbed person, a blamer and procrastinator who makes excuses or a proactive person in charge of your life?

Every word you speak says something about you. Your actions and their outcome also reflect what you speak and what you think. Use your vocabulary more consciously. As you do so, bear in mind that words can heal or hurt, build up or destroy, soothe or agitate, encourage or create despair, and debilitate or inspire progress.

Filter out the negative and defeating words. Wisely select those words that will help you and others to live a more productive, caring, joyful, fulfilling and peaceful life that every human heart desire.

6.

Speak Blessings into Your Life

You are here and now. So, this is the perfect moment for you to start speaking blessings into your life. It is a moment of realization that enough people are against you by wishing you misfortune. It is time to overpower this by blessing your life if you are losing focus and wasting time being too concerned about who is not on your side. If you believe in their hold over your life, you give power to it, and your life experience will unnecessarily feel as though it is one of continuous struggle.

Do not wait for others to bless your life. Bless your own as this is more powerful than their blessings. It is your life, not theirs. So, do not wait on others to wish you well. Then nobody's ill-thoughts, words, and actions against you can entrap you, and keep you down. Start declaring compelling and uplifting blessings into your life. You will begin to feel it is as true, and to see it manifesting for you.

Every day, be committed to consciously declare and speak into being goodness, graciousness, abundance, success, and beauty in your life, such as "I am enough." "I am whole, complete, and beautiful inside and out." "I am living an abundant and joyful life." "I am blessed with gifts and talents given to me by my Creator which I am using for my benefit, and to help others." "Life is beautiful." "I am growing from every obstacle as I flow around them, leaving them behind." "I declare victory into my life as I am allowing all things to work together for a greater good." "My Creator and I are for me so who can be against me?" When you make such declarations by speaking them aloud, they resonate on a subconscious level to manifest in reality, as they create a shift in you.

Today, as you step out into the world, do not wait for and depend on others to say something inspiring to you. Become self-sufficient as all these good things you want to hear already exist in you. Acknowledge them. Start saying beautiful, encouraging and uplifting words to yourself, so that your life becomes blessed and powerful.

7.

Become the Observer of Your Thoughts

It is a most beneficial exercise to become the watchful observer of your thoughts. Then you will be more aware of what they say, make you feel, speak and do. You are encouraged to spend at least ten minutes every day in silence and solitude so you could observe your thoughts, without which you would go about unconsciously expressing them verbally, and in your actions. You would begin to realize which thoughts uplift you, and which bring you down as you buy into them.

Never believe a thought that does not empower you, or your spirit and zeal will die. Treat every disempowering thought as a false belief, and it will lose power over you. Whatever you focus on materializes and grows. Every thought has power only when you buy into and focus on it, otherwise thought by itself is powerless. So, if you must hook on to a thought, hook on to empowering ones that will bring great benefit into your life such that it improves the quality of experience, and you evolve in nature and tendencies.

I recommend that from today start paying close

attention to your myriad of thoughts, and see how easy it is to get entangled in and identified with them, especially the disempowering ones. You might even start laughing at what transpires, as you watch them come and go.

This exercise will show you how you can take control of thought instead of it controlling you because you are deeply aware. In this way, you will not give power to defeating thoughts and those that create negative emotions, such as anger, hate, and deceit which harm you and when expressed in words and actions, inflict pain upon others. You will not give control over your life to anyone, or allow them to manipulate you because now you are very observant and can see clearly.

You are more powerful than you know. Take the reins on thought and become its master, so you can consciously choose empowering ones to steer your life in an enlightening and transformative direction.

8.

Let Success Be Your Best Revenge

When you experience adversity, it is easy to feel lost, hopeless and entrapped in a helpless position. It is, therefore, critical to take some time to go through the intensity of your inner pain to get relief, but not for too long, as there is no useful purpose in prolonging your suffering. The longer you take, the more you will struggle to get up, which delays you from moving forward in life. Instead, make adversity worth it by learning and growing from it to come out stronger, successful, and on top.

During adversity keep reminding yourself that you are growing up. You are developing understanding and willpower. Your character is building as you are being shaped and prepared to confidently move up to the next level, without which you would not be capable of doing what you are being called to do.

Adversity is a way to help one become humble and less judgmental of others. It is what will stir compassion and understanding to cause you to reach out and help another who is struggling. When you go through inner battles and come out of adversity, this is how Life allows you to inspire and help others from a place of authenticity.

So, when Life touches you and situations and events change you, always change for the better to make it worth it. Instead of staying bitter toward failure, adversity, and others see what knowledge and wisdom you have gained, as these will be the tools to use to help you soar. If you allow it, all things can come together to make a miracle out of mistakes. But this requires your co-operation and participation.

Just relax, refocus, strategize and get any help needed to move beyond adversity, as it is an avenue that Life uses to bring people together to support one another so we could become less selfish and more caring. Now you are well-positioned to turn adversity into opportunity.

Make success and enlightenment your best revenge ever, and you will see how your life will shine even brighter as you come out better not bitter. Life is filled with peaks and valleys. It is time to hit your peak once again. Do not miss out on this moment. You are ready.

9.

Generate a Belief That Works for Not Against You

There is a remarkable and dynamic interplay between belief and doubt. In reality, doubt is a belief; a belief against what you want. An interesting example that is quite common is that if you doubt you will ever be successful, then it means you believe that you will fail. In which case, you will be unable to see opportunities, and things will not work out and come together in the way you desire.

In other words, you are not only doubting that you will succeed, but you are also actually believing that you will fail. If you look closely at your words, attitude, actions, and results, they reflect this. Believe that you have failed and you suck the energy out of you. Believe that you learned lessons and you will generate energy to succeed. Such belief will fuel whatever you do and ignite a flame in you to never give up.

Whenever Life throws you for a loop, and you feel down and out, know that the only other place to go is up. All it requires is to shift your belief from the place to be is down to one that takes you up. Always remember that whatever you believe in, so shall Life bring to you. Start examining your doubt, and if that doubt is working against you, then start doubting that doubt, and generate a belief that works for you.

From this moment onward, discard all those beliefs that limit and constrict you and replace with beliefs that expand and grow you; and your life experience will change and improve. Change your programming by changing your inner dialogue with a new set of beliefs that empower you. To do so, start impressing upon your consciousness beliefs, such as "I am blessed," "I am a good soul," "I am compassionate and helpful," "I am creative," "I am skillful," "I am intelligent and productive," "I can, I will, I am doing and progressing."

Now make a list of empowering beliefs that work for you. Recite them every day, so they become natural to you, as part of your DNA. Notice the striking shift that takes place in your life.

10.

Stop the Self-Doubt

There is a saying that we are our worst enemy and our worst critic. Many people, however, do not understand the real truth behind this statement. Self-doubt is an unconscious defense mechanism used not to take the plunge, often to avoid doing something that you fear, as it may produce an unfavorable outcome, such as failure and disapproval. Self-doubt then becomes the excuse not to do what is necessary to go past one's fears and to explore possibilities. In this way, you make yourself your worst enemy as you work against you.

Self-doubt is you getting in your way to move ahead in life, as you question your ability and capability to produce a successful outcome. You believe that you are not good enough. In this way, you make yourself your worst critic. Self-doubt is when you also believe other people's doubts about you. Then use this as an excuse to blame them and situations instead of taking responsibility for your lack of progress. You unconsciously think that it is easier to blame than to step up for you.

It is time to stop the blame and self-doubt. Take back

your power from others and situations. Otherwise, life would pass you by unfulfilled and unhappy as you give up the chance to realize possibilities. You have amazing abilities and capabilities. Do not allow anyone to convince you otherwise. Just reach inside and tap into them and use them. As you do so continuously, you will energize them, and they will build momentum to thrust you forward.

Then one day, you will find yourself in a place, filled with confidence and humility that you didn't possess before, as you realize how far you have come from where you began. This applies in both the material and spiritual worlds. Discard all useless doubts. Retain your power. If anybody doubts you, doubt them.

Become your own best friend by believing in you and being kind to you. Do not waste any more time. Start using your abilities appropriately and wisely to enhance your experience and life would feel good, rewarding and satisfying.

11.

Keep Your Focus in the Right Place

Find that one thing that sparks you, that brings you alive, and you will find that it will move you instead of you forcing it to move. The key is to focus on what you can do, and as you give energy to this, you create momentum and fluidity. Eventually, you will find that creative solutions will surface for what you cannot do.

If you focus too much and for too long on what you cannot do, you will end up paralyzed in not doing. It is also beneficial that while you are doing—not to focus on how others are viewing you especially when it is unjustly negative—as you will have less time to focus on you and what you are doing. Keep your attention where it can prosper your life to create forward movement. It is, therefore, essential not to allow the inconsequential things, events, and people to distract you and waste your time so you could maintain focus in the right place.

Do not give unwarranted attention to defeats, as these will only make you feel discouraged. Instead focus on your victories—past, present, and future ones—because these will make you feel hopeful and full of eagerness, as they remind you of what you can achieve. Keep a balance between your abilities and challenges, and you will find that you do not have to force things to happen as flow will occur. When your current skills are below the level of your challenges approach them one at a time, and get help with those things that you cannot do, so you do not become overwhelmed. As you conquer a challenge, you would notice that your capabilities rose to meet the challenge, resulting in ongoing flow and progress.

The quality of your life depends upon where you position your focus and the degree of your attention. So, keep your focus steady in the right direction where you are inspired. Then you would feel transported to a marvelous place that you only dreamed about, but is finally here and now. The Indian sage named Patanjali expressed this idea very profoundly as follows:

> When you are inspired by some great purpose, some extraordinary project, all your thoughts break their bounds, your mind transcends limitations, your consciousness expands in every direction, and you find yourself in a new, great and wonderful world. Dormant forces, faculties, and talents become alive, and you discover yourself to be a greater person by far than you ever dreamed yourself to be.

12.

Open Your Own Door

It is interesting how some people sit and wait idly for a magical and fairyland door to open so that they could easily walk through it, only to realize that nothing is happening for them to get to where they dream of going. It is because they are waiting in their dreams, doing nothing in their reality to help it to unfold.

Sometimes, while you are looking for a door to open and cannot find one, there is a window that provides an opportunity to go through. All you need to do is change your perspective to see the potential and possibility that the window could provide. In other words, stay open. I have come to realize that if a door or window does not open up, then carve out one. Push it open and go through it with faith, surrender and a sense of adventure, without which it would feel difficult to go through the door that you are carving out.

Often, Life requires you to find the power within, as it wants your co-operation, effort and willingness to make the most of what you have and can do. Then Life bestows upon you the resources to help you get to where you want to go, which when these arrive often feel like grace. It feels like grace because they can show up when least expected, and in unexpected ways. To keep these flowing in, you need to make the most of the grace by using its gifts to the fullest, and with immense gratitude. Otherwise, they can dissipate. It is also crucial to recognize which resources are useful as some time-wasting ones may come disguised as candy, which can set you back and even be destructive. Stay alert, pay attention to your gut feeling combined with rationale, and take the best action possible under the given circumstances.

Always remember during the times when you are carving out your door, and when no doors or windows are opening up, that to everything there is a season and a time for everything. There is a time when a door shuts behind you because that experience is over and something new ahead is for you. If you keep trying to re-open that shut door, you will miss out on what awaits you. If you pry it open and re-enter, do not be surprised if you get forced out. In which case, Life is telling you that it is time for something else.

There is a time when a door shuts in your face because it is not the one for you, and there is no window to go through because you need some pruning where you are before you could move on. So, do not be disappointed. Be patient as you are being protected. There is a time for something to die, to give way for the birth of something new; a time to keep and a time to throw away; a time to tear down and a time to rebuild; a time to plant, a time to grow and a time to pluck joyfully and with wisdom.

Recognize and understand what time and season you are in, so you will struggle less and grow to allow you to move on.

13.

Start the Best Detox Program

Start your best detox program today. Detox from all the false and disempowering beliefs and conditioning that you have accumulated thus far to hold you back, and darken your inner and outer worlds. Some of the conditioning can be fruitful when it encourages, motivates and inspires. It is the type you keep and enhance. There is, however, another type of conditioning that can often be damaging to your well-being. It is the type that has a negative influence because of its limiting effects to which you need to pay close attention and start examining.

Eliminate and detach inwardly from negative people with restrictive ideas and concepts. Disassociate from energy suckers and toxic environments that steal your joy. It is wise to become ever aware of your external environment because if its negative energy is more than your positive energy, it will begin to contaminate your internal environment to make you become like it, and those in it.

When you start your detox, be firm about eliminating the influence of your energy suckers but do not be deliberately mean toward them. Otherwise, this would make you negative like them. As you get rid of these toxins, you will begin to feel truly clean, and alive inside. Like every detox program, once you eradicate all the toxins, you must replace them with what is healthy. Do not detox and stay in isolation, at least not for too long, as this can eventually and easily dull you.

Start aligning with inspiring energy generators, as together the energy builds, which will increase your energy and what you do. Be an energy builder instead of an energy vampire. Start being all that you know you can be and do. You can be kind. You can be considerate. You can be generous and helpful. You can be resourceful. You can be joyful. You can reach the heights that you are born to attain as you have it in you to do it.

14.

Let People Go

Do you tend to hold on to people who do not want you in their lives, and them in yours? Whenever people leave you, do not beg them to stay based on unfounded reasons, such as neediness. Bless them to go their way as they are not part of your future, your destiny. Otherwise, they would be here with you. They are not going where you are going, and if they are, they have decided to use another route. So, wish them well as you will be more empowered to greet them respectfully yet detached, if and whenever next you meet up.

For now, they have served their purpose and no longer have staying power. Let them go otherwise it would feel "hard" on the inside, as you strive to keep them around. Sometimes, it is best to let people go as you have no common bond. Your values, principles, beliefs, and interests are no longer aligned.

If you hold on to them, their influence will erode your drive for life, and deter you from where you want to go and be. If, however, they are precious to you, such as your family, then do not give up on them even if they have given up on you. Show them that you care about them, as you never know what challenge or inner battle they may be undergoing. In doing so, you must be a safe and trusting place for them, without which they will not be able to embrace you.

Generally, if people do not have time for you, it is an indicator of how important you are to them, and of what value. In other words, currently, you are unimportant and of no value to them. It does not mean that you are valueless. It is just that they do not need you and neither do they care about you in the way they did. Otherwise, they would check in on you at least for a few minutes at reasonable intervals. There is no need to mope for them, nor feel sorry for yourself, because while you are sulking over losing them, they are not doing the same for you. They are not missing you. They are busy living their lives without you.

Move on without being bitter and get busy living your life without them. Liberate yourself from inner suffering by releasing them. Be thankful that you were used as a worthy instrument to be there for them and they for you, as they served a useful purpose at that time. So never discredit them. This viewpoint of appreciation will leave you feeling light and free.

The time and space these people once occupied in your life are now available for you to explore endless possibilities. Soon, you wouldn't notice that they are gone as you are busy living, and one day you would look back and wonder why is it you ever thought that you still needed them. Now you have the room available for the new and right people to enter your life who are going where you want to go and are using the same track that you are on. All else is dead-weight that will drag you down. You are stronger than you think. Keep moving forward.

15.

Stand Out on Strength

Observe life. You would notice how easy it is to stand out only by putting others down or measuring yourself against those whom you believe are weaker than you. It is the only way you can feel you are great. It is in fact, great weakness. If you want to examine how you are doing and must measure yourself against others, at least be brave enough to do so against those whom you perceive are above you. Then you can pull yourself up to a higher standard.

If, however, you can stand out brilliantly on your own worth and character, this is strength. Likewise, when you praise someone do so based on their merit, character, ability, and realized potential instead of comparing them to another person who is weaker. Otherwise, you would be devaluing your compliment to them, and therefore, you would not be honoring their true worth.

People's sense of greatness is a fiction of their imagination. It is the way they create self-importance at others' expense who buy into it. If you base your self-worth on those whom you perceive is below you, then there is not much merit to it. To determine your true worth, measure yourself against your weaknesses and see how much stronger you have grown from these, and how far you have come.

This message is asking you to stand out on your own strength, not on another's weakness and humbly help someone find their worth. In the process, your character and value will increase exponentially.

16.

Make Some Lemonade

Rest assured that whatever Life throws your way, you have the option to take the lemons of life and make lemonade. Now you can proceed to live. I wish I could assure you that you could have a pain-free life and that everything would go smoothly for you at all times but as you know this is not so.

The reality is that at some point in our lives each of us will experience loss, disappointment or adversity in some form. Life will always find a reason to send a challenge in your path because when you get uncomfortable, this is what will help you to grow, transform and evolve. Without discomfort, there will be a tendency to stay at the level you are at, which stunts your growth.

While you cannot always control what happens to you, you get to decide today that from now on what is in your control is how you interpret and perceive what Life sends you, and how you choose to respond to it and what you do with it. Do you see failure as a person or an event? Do you see something as not working out as defeat or as an opportunity for something better? Do you see a loss as devastating or as making room for something new and worthwhile to gain? Do you see a fall as an end to all or as something small from which you can rise tall?

Before you rush off to make lemonade with the lemons that Life throws at you, take some time to taste the bitterness, as it is a means to cleanse you. Premature positivity means that you have negativity lurking in the background, which can erupt at any time to destroy you, and others.

It is, therefore, wise to carve out some specific time to feel your loss or disappointment deeply, so that these negative energies do not get lodged in your body to create illness and negative emotions, which you can easily project unto others irrationally, and at inappropriate times. Too often, too many people ignore and fail to go through this process, and to their detriment.

When you have dealt with the negativities, you can flush them totally out of your system by adding the sweetness of wisdom to the lemons of Life to make lemonade. Now you can truly enjoy life and be pleasant company.

17.

See Value in Aloneness

Right now, you may be feeling alone. Nobody is there for you. You are all by yourself. You feel used, discarded, abandoned, shunned and ghosted by family, friends, bosses, associates, society, and even by God. I want you to feel assured that this will not last forever, as the power of aloneness is in your hands.

The secret to overcoming aloneness is to make it work for you rather than viewing it as poor pitiful me, which works against you. Start by not giving power to complaining and defeating thoughts, such as "I must be bad," "nobody loves me or cares for me," "I am not good enough for them," "they no longer need me," "I am not important to them," and "nobody is there for me and wants to help me."

Understand, accept and honor the fact that people change and their needs change at various stages in life just like yours do, except that theirs are now different to yours. It is not necessarily a reflection that something is wrong with you but a change in them and where they are. If something is wrong, then this is the perfect moment to address it and make things right in you. This time of aloneness is a sacred gift to you to empower you. It is an opportunity to discover who you are, what you want to do, and where you want to go without other people's influence and impressions upon you.

So, use your alone time well. It is an opportunity to focus one hundred percent of your efforts on creating the kind of life you want; a transformed, healed, and vibrant one filled with clarity, purpose, and strength. While it is important not to feel lonely when you are alone, or with others, it is also equally important not to be alone in this massive world. On a practical level, you need to have others close to you for safety reasons and in the case of sudden illness or other emergency situations. So be wise about being alone.

Instead of feeling alone and deserted, seek out and align with people who are engaged in making a positive difference in the world, and something in which you are interested. Help somebody who needs a helping hand. In the end, you would find that you are not alone and while others have abandoned you, you have not given up on yourself.

See your alone time as an immense blessing, for without it you would not have considered moving to live closer to loved ones, or kindling new relationships. You would not have discovered new opportunities, resilience, deep faith, and a sense of self, which is the principal purpose behind aloneness. This book was birthed out of a period of alone time. It is how I channeled my time and energy away from feeling sorry for myself, and toward a greater understanding of life that I could share with others. You could do something similar, too.

18.

Stop Feeling Sorry for Yourself

You probably need to have a good cry. Go ahead and let it all out. Feel sorry for yourself for a few minutes, an hour or a day, but not for too long. Now stop the sulking because it will not change or make things any better. Okay, something didn't turn out the way you hoped. You are disappointed. You feel like a failure, and that others have failed you. Be consoled. You are not alone. A whole planet of people is on your side. They, too, know what that is like, as every human being has gone through such an experience at some point. And yes, that includes even those who consider themselves to be giants and geniuses.

Now it is time to stop feeling sorry for yourself. Start counting your blessings by looking for something for which you can be grateful every single day. Go ahead, force it out. You will find it even if it is the fact that this morning you woke up and can breathe while there are others who are supported by an oxygen tank, or you have clean water to drink when many others do not even have access to clean running water. You have the ability to read and write when there are so many who never had the opportunity to learn to do so or the convenience of a washroom which is a luxury for many in other parts of the world.

One of the best ways to also stop feeling sorry for yourself, which is a reflection of your gratitude is to reach out and help someone who needs a helping hand in an area that you can provide. As you touch that person and he or she lights up, you would begin to brighten up, too.

In the process, when you make a positive difference in someone's life, you end up making a positive difference in yours. It is the space in which you begin to feel hopeful and more expansive. It is here you feel inspired to find solutions for whatever didn't work out in your life. Take measures to implement and make a change, and humbly yet assertively ask for help. You would be surprised at how much help you would eventually draw toward you.

Look at the bright side of things, as there are always two sides of a coin. Perk up, and things would start looking up, and life would begin to feel exhilarating.

19.

Press Pause Then Reset

At this moment, if you are feeling confused or lost, then it is the right time to press pause. Many people may be influencing your life and choices. You may be extremely overwhelmed by regret. You may be feeling as though you faltered along the way and are off-course due to poor decisions made, although based on good intentions.

Be gentle with yourself. Life is not over until your last breath. Take a break from everything and everyone so that you could stop stifling and breathe evenly, examine where you are, and where you truly want to be. Only then can you press reset.

I want to assure you that as long as you have breath you have life and as long as you are alive you have another chance. You no longer need to sit on the sidelines beating up on yourself and others, and living in guilt, condemnation, and hopelessness.

To get back on track, find a quiet and sacred place where you could be alone in silence so that you could pay attention and listen to what your inner voice says, which requires you to drop all preconceived ideas. Then there is stillness, calmness, and spaciousness within from where you could quietly determine what you want, and be at peace with it. Now you can press reset.

From every mistake, good can come out of it if you were to stay open to learn from it. The key is to leave it in the past, and embrace what the future has to offer by doing your best with what you have now. The more you learn, the more wisdom you gain and can share with others.

Press pause, then reset with a fresh plan, charting out a new course to head in the direction you would like to go. Give life another chance and allow a mistake to turn into something magnificent in your world.

20.

Turn Regret into Now I Know

It is not unusual to go through life having regrets because not everything you do will turn out the way you want it. What you do with these, however, is what makes the big difference in your experience.

Right now you may be filled with remorse, deep regret, and pain for something you did or did not do. To cover up your regret which is lurking in the background, you may be distracting yourself with lots of activities and engagements. There is no need to do this anymore. The time has arrived for you to finally put your regret to rest, so that it does not suck luster out of you, and keep you trapped in a debilitating place.

Life is about making choices and taking actions with no guarantee of a particular outcome in most cases. Everybody makes choices and usually with the best of intentions, and within their capacity. These choices and actions are based on the knowledge and wisdom you possess at that time. If something did not work out favorably be gentle with yourself. Instead of perceiving it as deep regret, turn it around in your favor by saying to yourself that you no longer have to wonder about "what if," as now you know. Then you have the power to forgive yourself for what you deemed a mistake.

You can fix what you can by making different choices and taking different actions, and again with good intentions and faith. Like the Serenity Prayer says, "Accept the things you cannot change, have the courage to change the things you can, and the wisdom to know the difference." So, see your regret as "Now I Know" and therefore, "Now I Can, Differently."

If anyone says that they have no regrets despite poor decisions and choices that produced unfavorable results, and affected others in detrimental ways, then they are unconscionable. When you have regrets, it means you have recognized and accepted that your actions produced undesirable results, and while you cannot undo what was done, it is from here that you can take corrective action going forward. In this, there is no longer darkness or debilitation, but clear vision, forward motion, and freedom as regret gets transformed into realization.

21.

Be Patient

There are universal laws of nature that are at play in every aspect of creation. One of such laws is that there is a gestation period needed for growth and manifestation and that everything happens in its own time, not yours.

There is a profound reason why a gestation period is required, and it is all about what you do during this time. Gestation requires patience. Patience is about your attitude while you are waiting. Observe nature. Consider the lilies how they grow as they toil not [force not, stress not], and spin not [do not keep changing their mind, or worry] and yet they grow.

This gestation period is a growing up period for you, as much as, it is a birthing period for what you want. To grow, you must pay attention to lessons that reveal themselves and learn from them by applying their principles. Stay committed and do not give up. Do not keep changing your mind if it is something you truly want and believe in otherwise, it will not manifest, and you will get nowhere close to it despite your many wavering efforts. Such patience gives birth to an understanding person who accepts the universal laws of nature, as you surrender to and have faith in its process.

The gestation period is the time that the universal laws of nature give to you to become like the lilies and be at ease in yourself. It is the time given to you to find joy during the process, and to be grateful for everything and everyone that show up along the way, and not wait merely for that one moment when the thing you want arrives. Why settle for one moment of joy when you could have so much joy throughout the journey? It is a principle of Life and one of its many lessons.

As you co-operate with the laws of nature by applying the lessons learned, the gap between your focused attention, consistent and persistent actions, and what you want begins to close. Become like the lily along the way, and you will be a more pleasant person to be around. Then others will want to join you for the ride.

22.

Handle Critics as Though They Do Not Exist

One of the greatest human desires is to be liked and to receive approval from others; to know that one is good enough and is somebody worthwhile in the eyes of others; to know that one is accepted and has a sense of belonging and relevance through validation from others. To know that one matter in this vast universe. All of which can, unfortunately, lead to a lack of self-confidence, inferiority complexes, unhealthy choices, and set up for criticism.

Anywhere you turn, somebody is criticizing somebody for some reason. If you are not careful and you give too much attention to this, it would stunt your progress and happiness. Stay focused on your life and what you do, and be ever alert in how you are doing it so that it is constructive and does not intentionally hurt anyone.

In the process, know that when you do good, there will be those who praise you and critics who condemn you. When you do wrong, there will be people who defend and want to help you reform and critics who want to punish you.

When you succeed, there will be some who put you on a pedestal and critics who negatively critique you. When you fail, there are those who uplift you and others who revel in your downfall. There are also those who will think you are somebody today and those same people will think you are nobody tomorrow. So, treat critics who want to bring you down as though they do not exist. Then they cannot have power, influence, and control over you. If you give in to your critics, they feel good not you.

Critics who condemn are miserable because of their negativity, of which they are unconscious. Misery likes company so they criticize you with the hope that you will become miserable, too. The best strategy is to turn a blind eye to them. Direct your energy and attention to do good and succeed, as this will cause your life to flourish, and make you feel good and alive inside. On the other hand, your critics waste their time, efforts and thoughts in negativity that keep alive their misery.

You have something to contribute to the world that is amazing. Just believe in yourself. Each day offers a fresh start. Do good as it is natural to you. It has immense credibility in it that validates you. It says that you are alright and doing just fine, which is nobody's business, only yours.

23.

Do Not Get Lost in Anger

The ability to pay attention to life is a priceless gift that you can give to yourself. When you start to notice, it is when you can see clearly and make changes as needed. It is from here that a significant shift can occur in your state of being. Many people are angry and believe that it is normal and even acceptable to be angry and to blame others for their anger. Without realizing it anger becomes a constant factor in one's life that erupts explosively at any time, and often without warning, as left unattended it can be triggered by the slightest stimulus.

When you find yourself amidst angry people, remember to treat their anger as exactly so; it is theirs. As such, whenever anyone gets angry at you to be aware that this is their stuff—not yours—and that they are ill-treating and beating up themselves by being angry. If you get back angry at them, you make their stuff your stuff. Practice becoming consciously aware in every moment when anger arises, so that you do not get drawn into and lost in other people's world, and get infected and affected by them.

If you do not like certain people's behaviors and attitudes, such as their anger, do not react negatively and explosively to them otherwise, you have allowed them to make you become like them; the very thing you do not like. Anger is abuse to oneself. It is abusive to another when the person is not consciously aware and absorbs it and allows it to affect them by reacting angrily. Stay alert and pay attention to your reactions. Cultivate a clean and healthy inner world, and then you will be able to become compassionate toward an angry person without getting caught up in their anger.

Understand that when someone is angry, they are already in pain. They need help and counseling. They, therefore, do not need you to inflict more pain by reacting in the same way as them. It does not mean that you allow them to ill-treat you. Be firm with them if needed, but do not become like them. If you, too, become angry it means an alarm is going off. It is waking you up to fix something in you that needs to be addressed.

To go beyond anger begins with you becoming consciously aware of it to control it, so you do not express it irresponsibly. You do not try to manage it. Why manage that which is not good? You manage what you want to keep and eliminate what you do not like. To do so, you need help to identify its origin, understand its source and reason, accept life's happenings, feel its pain deeply once and for all, forgive to transcend and become free of anger, to go into an inner space of peace.

You are superior to and above anger so do not allow it to control you, as you are love, compassion, understanding, and graciousness.

24.

Be for You

When the world is against you, make sure you are the one person who is for you. Not everybody will seek your interest, and nobody can do so at all times because they have to take care of themselves, too. Be interested in your well-being without wilfully hurting others in the process. If you feel nobody is for you, then you are not for you. And, if you are not for you do not have the unrealistic expectation of others being there for you.

People will make well-intended promises to you. Many will get broken to cause you to lose trust in them. Dreams will get shattered, and life will at times feel broken. Since life is unpredictable and people and circumstances change continuously, it is not the place to put your trust. Be for you and trust in a higher power to guide you to help you to remain open to others and the wonder of life. Otherwise, you would miss out on what it has to offer.

If and when the world takes everything away from you, do not let it take away your inner substance, too. It is yours and what you will need to rebuild. Stay alert to this as it is an essential survival tool in the midst of challenges. When others are saying "No" to your life, you stand up and say "Yes" to it. Do not wait for others to be for you. You be for you, and your inner world will become like a magnet drawing in all that is good and beneficial.

Do not undervalue your abilities by relying too heavily upon others to energize you, and keep you going. You are made up of energy. Use it and let it accelerate in your favor. You are blessed with immense favor, talents, gifts, courage, resilience, faith, intuition, creativity, intelligence, skills, and much more. Recognize these in yourself and use them well to say "Yes" to your life. Then Life and others will surprise you as they start saying "Yes" back to you. Be your number one cheerleader, and run your race to the finish line. Be for you.

25.

Forgive to Become Free

To forgive is one of the most liberating, loving thing you can do for yourself. It is the door through which guilt, anger, hurt, resentment, disappointment, and frustration can walk freely out of your life, as higher understanding enters. The one who hurts the most through un-forgiveness is you, as it ties you to pain and to those whom you do not revere, which holds you back.

Understand that everybody makes mistakes, and acts only based on where they are within themselves, that is, the knowledge, wisdom, and understanding they have at that point in their lives. That is all you can get out of a human being. When you do not forgive, it becomes your excuse to be a victim, anchored in a dark and hurtful place, and chained to the past.

Be courageous. Take responsibility for your happiness. Set yourself free from the shackles of hurt, so you do not lose years of enjoying life to its fullest. Otherwise, you are allowing un-forgiveness to be your crutch to stay miserable and stuck. To forgive others you have to forgive yourself first. Why? As long as you have not forgiven others, you are hurting yourself and are creating pain in you through your hurt, anger, or disappointment in them. When you forgive yourself, you have a pure, inner environment from where you can truly forgive others.

Now you know better, you can do better. Forgive and forget so you can heal. To forget does not mean to remove from memory. If you delete from memory, you will blindly and unconsciously allow yourself to get hurt again in the same way. To forget means not to hold on to any negativity. It requires you to be in your original state of being before you got hurt where there was no feeling of anger, disappointment or bitterness, although you come out a changed person. Now you are wiser, stronger and more aware instead of unhappy and weak.

Cut your identity to the umbilical cord of pain. Decide to forgive. Let divine wisdom work through you by keeping your heart and mind open to bring deep understanding in, so that its grace releases you from the burden of unforgiveness. To enjoy freedom, bless the one who has hurt you, as you get to experience the sacred power in forgiving. Bless them so that they would one day come to know better so they, too, could become free within. The world will be a much better and loving place in which to live.

Use today to forgive or say you are sorry as it is a humble recognition of erring ways that will set you free from the bondage of pain. To err is human, to forgive makes us divine, and that is beautiful, loving and peaceful.

26.

Use a New Yardstick of Measurement

Be confident. Pull out a new yardstick of measurement; yours. If you want to examine how you are doing in life never measure yourself against others. If you do, you will set yourself up to feel like a failure or end up with an unattractive ego. There will always be greater or lesser persons than yourself. Do not let anyone define success for you as this can be different for everyone. Define this based on what it means to you, not others.

Even those who label themselves as giants and geniuses fail in some area of their lives. It is because what makes them a giant or genius in a particular area is the fact that they focused most of their attention on the area in which they excelled. With little attention directed to other areas of their lives, those areas suffer, and they experience failure. So, do not be misguided into believing that the self-proclaimed giants and geniuses are brilliant in all areas of their lives. They may be a genius in one area and just average or even fail in another.

If you must measure yourself, do so only against your capabilities, abilities, and potential. From here you will know what you need to do to measure up, without having to feel less than any other person. In this way, you can maintain joy and balance in your life. Your idea of genius may be average to another person, and that person's idea of genius may be average to somebody else. It all depends upon what each person wants to be happy and at peace. So, get your own yardstick of measurement. If you decide to measure yourself against others, do so not to compare, but a means to lift your potential to a higher level.

During your challenging times, bear in mind that the measure of a person is not determined by what one is going through. Nor is it by the fact that one gets up but how one gets up, that is, the values used to ascend, which reflect the quality of the human being who gets up.

In the end, one's equanimity through both success and failure is a reflection of the substance of a person. It is what Life is calling upon each of us to achieve. This is real success. Most people, however, miss this point as they focus primarily on the external result exclusive of one's state of being as the indicator of success.

Let us stop beating each other down and being less judgmental and come together, value and respect each other's efforts, and where possible inspire, encourage and help one another attain the higher level to which we are striving.

27.

Use Your Fall as Your Launchpad

It is not how many times you fall that counts but the fact that you got up each time. In the same way, it does not matter how many punches Life throws at you, but how many you can take. When you fall, it is only a stumble that keeps you humble, not a failure.

When you fall, there may be different reasons to why somebody else fell in the same way as you did. Likewise, when people tell you that you keep going around the same mountain expecting different results, do not just buy into it. Examine it as it relates to you as it may have a different meaning for you. Sometimes, when you fall it may or may not mean that you are doing something wrong, or in the wrong way, or that it is not for you.

In such a situation, Life could be testing your grit, stamina, and strength of character; how much you want what you want; how much you believe in you and what you want; and whether or not you have what it takes to handle what you want when you get it. As such, you may have to go around the same mountain a few times, get knocked out and get back up each time. The key is to stay open so you can determine which lesson applies to you, and what you need to do to get the results you want.

So when you fall, do not give up. Instead, use it as your Launchpad to blast off. You have to start somewhere, or you will get nowhere. When you start at the bottom where you fell, one day you will be able to look back and see how far you have come and grown, and that is precious and humbling.

Now you are strategically positioned not to feel as though you are above others while you use your experience to help those who are at the bottom to realize that they, too, have it in them to blast off. What a splendid way to live, and be.

28.

Deal with Criticism Gracefully

The ability to stay open and humble to listen to a well-intended critique about oneself is a beautiful quality in any human being. There is wisdom in paying attention to criticism as it is the portal to evolving when the critique can enhance areas, such as one's attitude, behavior, approach, choices, skills, and character.

Not all criticisms, however, have significance as these could be just somebody's opinion. Everybody has a right to their opinions based on their perceptions, influences, knowledge, and wisdom, or lack of these. It is imperative to have the fortitude and deep insight to be able to discern whether or not the criticism is useful to you, and has anything to teach you. Your ability to not feed negative criticism by not reacting negatively like a victim is a reflection of an individual who knows how to live gracefully. In doing so, it does not mean that you cannot stand up for yourself.

Often, you are affected when criticized, not only by what is said but also by the tone of delivery and articulation. After the initial punch of criticism, it is advisable to look at it honestly and objectively to see if there is something that you need to change in you. If there is, then make the change that is needed as it is for your improvement. If the criticism has no validity, then disregard it and stay joyful within. In both cases, you come out a victor.

The ultimate purpose of every person's existence is to evolve by becoming a better, more joyful, loving, peaceful and blissful being. So never miss out on an opportunity to transform. Deal with criticism humbly. You will feel like a beautiful and graceful human being, and others will view you as such.

29.

Start Somewhere or You Will Get Nowhere

People tend to believe that everything must be perfect and that they must begin perfectly positioned to achieve a goal that they would like to attain. One reason for this may be because they want to escape criticism. Thus, they often become procrastinators never feeling ready or good enough.

They may also have an illusory belief that successful people begin perfectly or may have created a false idea to sabotage their take-off for fear of failure. As such, time flies by as they fail to launch, never reaching their full potential. Their perfectionism takes them in a direction opposite to where they want to go, which leaves them unhappy.

Successful people usually begin imperfectly with little or no support and enhance things as they go along, which comes from making mistakes. Because they do not view these as a failure, they do not get stuck in mistakes but learn and grow from them which allow progress. Instead of waiting for a perfect moment, they take a moment and make it the perfect one from which to start.

Life deliberately calls upon us to begin imperfectly. It is so that we can stay humble, open to learn and grow along the way, savor the experience of learning, and appreciate the goal on its attainment. When we start-off imperfectly, we are in a better position to not judge and condemn others. Instead, we have understanding, compassion and a greater willingness to help with patience.

I have come to respect this saying by Bob Marley, “If you don’t start somewhere, you gonna get nowhere.” So, start now from where you are, imperfectly. Give the best you have to offer at that point in time. Keep moving as it will get you somewhere. If you stop, you will get nowhere notable. As you keep doing, you will improve with practice to leave your distinct imprint in this world.

30.

Choose Your Battles Wisely

Everything in which you engage requires energy, your energy. Either you expend your energy wastefully, or you invest it in such a way as to bring you an invaluable return. Often people engage in useless battles where they waste time and energy fighting with others, and in the end, they fight with themselves as they lose their spirits and joy, when they could have used the same time and energy to live a more rewarding life.

This is often evident in the case where there is a death, and families spend so much time, energy and money battling with each other for family heirlooms. These are only things to which they have attached more importance than the relationship they have with each other. Each person has gifts and talents in which they could invest their time and energy to acquire those things of which they could be proud, and to which they could assign importance, instead of having to rely on heirlooms that they did not work to earn.

Such families could have more wisely used their energy to share the heirlooms in an equitable and fair manner to maintain harmony in the relationships. It would save a lot of time, energy, money, and the relationship they have with each other. They end up being bitter as their energies are misplaced and they lose their spark and enthusiasm while fighting against others.

If you are fighting a battle, stop for a while and ask yourself these pertinent questions. "What will you lose including your energy and time?" "What will you gain and will it be more than your loss?" "How is your state of mind affected and how is it impacting those close to you?" "How else could you use your time, energy and money to bring you far superior gains that will allow you to maintain inner balance, and overall advancement?"

Realize where you are wasting and depleting your energy, your vital life-force. You are now being called upon to redirect your energy by investing it in something more beneficial, whereby you are using your gifts and talents to enrich your life and other people's life; to prosper it and promote harmony. You deserve the best that Life has to offer so do not settle for less.

31.

Be a Wise Example

A wise leader encourages and brings out the leader in others, as it serves to benefit all involved. A wise leader is not insecure but confident and knows that there is a piece of pie for everybody in this vast universe. A wise leader does not count oneself a leader, but an outstanding example that inspires and brings out the best in others by helping them to see the best and realize a great potential in themselves.

If everybody is a leader then, there is nobody to follow. As such, it is time to reshape the leadership concept. It is time now to step up to a higher standard. Be an outstanding example by your attitudes, behaviors, speech, actions, and choices whereby you encourage togetherness instead of, selfishness. In doing so, it does not mean to allow others to take advantage of you and situations. Although, it may require you to use intelligent discrimination within reason for the sake of all concerned.

A person who is a wise example does not waste time in blame and condemnation, but takes responsibility to make a difference given time, place and circumstance. Such a person is open to fail and learn from it; to succeed and share;

to bring others together in a co-operative spirit instead of dividing to conquer; as such a person truly understands with wisdom that everybody is living life, and wants to get the best out of it.

Today, as you assume and engage in your various roles challenge yourself to be a remarkable example not to impress others, but because this is the potential released out of you. Then others will naturally notice you for the right reason. Be what you want to see and get out of others, and the world. You have it in you to be a wise example even in the smallest role. Turn on the light of wisdom in you and let it shine through.

32.

Change Your Perspective on Failure

Firstly, failure is not a person and therefore is not you, but an outcome. It is not the end of the world. It is not the end of your life or opportunities, abilities, and capabilities. It is just something not working out favorably for you when and how you expected, either due to an approach you used, timing, or somebody`s subjective opinion. With this perspective, you can start overcoming failure. All you need to do is to realize that failure is only an instrument to deliver a message to you.

The message may be not as yet, not the right time, not the right thing or person; something else or someone else is for you; chart a new course; different approach required; need other tools; more preparation, knowledge, skill sets or wisdom needed; and learn some lessons. It also alerts you to look out, bumpy road ahead while learning and navigating through new and different territory for a smooth landing.

Stay open to decode and receive what message is before you. Decipher it and use it to your advantage so you can shift from failure to a new plan, and as the saying goes turn a setback into a setup for a comeback. In other words, your knockdown is the perfect platform from which to become a knockout, as it shows the courage and stamina you possess to rise up.

My dad taught me that when a door closes another one opens, which I found was the case when I kept this type of influence. Whenever I kept company with those who believed otherwise by viewing something not working out as devastating, my world came tumbling down as I felt I failed.

As such, to keep the right perspective, it is necessary to keep the right influence who will remind you that when a door closes, it has served its purpose and that chapter of your life is over, and something more appropriate and better is in store for you.

Success is heading your way. Believe in yourself as new doors are opening, new opportunities are coming your way. Obstacles are being pushed out as you are learning, growing and getting prepared to receive what is for you. Just stay open, reposition, formulate a new plan, execute as needed, and enjoy the ride which is a success in itself.

33.

Value Your Relationships

At the end of this journey called your life, unless you are a very unconscious human being, you would realize that your relationships are an invaluable possession. As such, nurture them and do not take them for granted because at a moment's notice life can be snatched away.

On your death-bed, you would not be asking for all the things that you accomplished and acquired as these only serve a practical purpose on earth. You would be asking for the people whom you claim to love and love you. Their nearness is what would provide you with comfort, closeness, and support.

In this modern world, where many gurus are convincing people to go after their passion and achieve the purpose that they are here to fulfill, they are losing sight of what is truly precious in life. Your passion and purpose are never merely about the fulfillment of these things, but about how you grow and evolve through these in terms of your relationship with yourself, and others.

It is never too late to start re-evaluating where you have anchored your value. As such, this is the right time to weigh what you are willing to lose when you are pursuing your dreams exclusive of valuing your relationships by nurturing them. Show people you care and that they matter by not neglecting and depreciating them, but by including them. Healthy relationships can bring much joy to your life experience and to what you achieve.

Always bear in mind, that in a relationship it is not about who is right and who is wrong. The one who steps up first to do the right thing, to heal and create harmony in oneself, and in the relationship is the powerful one. So, wisely nurture and cherish your relationships, and be a powerhouse and step up together.

34.

Keep a Grateful Heart

One of the most superior ways to keep your spirits alive especially during challenging times is to keep finding reasons every morning and throughout your day to be grateful. As you see your blessings even in the smallest things and ways, you will find that they improve your mood to produce energetic thoughts of enthusiasm. As your enthusiasm comes alive, you will begin to feel more and more hopeful. Your courage will grow, and this strength will uplift you when you are down.

When you stay in a place of gratitude, it becomes the fertile seed planted in your heart, out of which sprouts the shoots of creative thoughts of possibilities that bear the fruit of progress. Gratitude can be likened to a lightbulb as it shines brightly over darkness to bring hope, clarity, and vision. As such, a grateful heart can never be kept down but instead, gives you wings to fly and soar.

Deliberately introduce gratitude into your life every day and notice the difference it makes. You could do so by writing your gratitude. When you see it, it stands out, and you feel it on a deeper level. This record could also serve as a source of things for which you could be grateful if ever you run out of gratitude in the future. Another way is to say it out loud because every spoken word has energy, which is powerful than merely writing it. As you say it, you start to feel it and believe it as true.

The stronger the belief, the greater the vibration of your spoken gratitude and the higher you are uplifted. Thus, you become more energized to move forward. You could also express your gratitude by doing kind deeds and telling others how grateful you are to them, which makes them feel appreciated. It creates a boost in your happy hormone to help you maintain a positive attitude.

Start declaring your gratitude. "I am thankful for my family." "I am thankful for this day as it gives me another chance to make things better for my life." "I am grateful for the food I eat and clean water to drink." "I am so thankful for the fresh air I breathe." "I appreciate having at least one person on my side as it gives me the strength and courage to keep going." "I am grateful that I got an opportunity to be kind to somebody today." "I am very thankful that I can see all my blessings as they feed me with hope to make enormous headway." Be grateful and what seemed impossible will look possible and brilliant ideas will surface.

35.

Get Out of Your Own Way

If you are stuck in some area of your life, it could be that you need to get out of your own way. Sometimes to get out of your own way, you also have to get others out of your way, as they impose their limiting beliefs, negative criticisms, and opinions of you that you unconsciously absorb, and embrace as your own. It means that you may have to cut or limit ties with these people. You will also have to stop listening to the voice in your head with all its disempowering beliefs.

Ask yourself some profound questions to bring clarity upon the real reasons why you are stuck. Are you stuck because you are unwilling to do what others do to get ahead? Are you using other people's limiting beliefs of you as your excuse to remain in an unfulfilling situation, so you do not have to do anything but have complaints? Are you stuck because you are being asked to do something that is out of alignment with who you are? Are you scared of failing as things may not work out in the way you hope and that you will be judged? Now ask yourself, "How long do you plan on staying pinned to a pitiful position when you have much to offer?"

The only way to get unstuck is to adopt a new set of beliefs that empower, and not defeat. Get a new circle of influence that motivates, stimulates, encourages, inspires and provide real solutions and direction. Most importantly, stop complaining and making excuses. Go beyond your fears and limitations because only those who risk going too far can find out how far they can really go.

Start doing that which resonates with you. When you disable all the limiting beliefs and influences, all that is left is for you to get up. Nothing will change until you move. So get up and start moving. Do not wait on others to motivate you. Motivate yourself as this is for your benefit, not theirs.

Go ahead and jump; spring forward with no obsessive over-thinking. Take a leap of faith. Do not miss out on what you are meant to have, and be. When you get it, make it even more breathtaking by sharing with others and paying homage to those who helped you along the way.

36.

See Fear as a Messenger

A person's greatest fear is often fear itself. Fear is a natural emotion given to us by creation to use with wisdom, not to perpetuate it. Fear is an emotional mechanism designed to get one's attention as it triggers a message to become alert of possible danger ahead, and could be indicating to you not to approach, at least not as yet.

It is an intense feeling that can debilitate and prevent you from getting what you want in the silence of your heart, and from being happy often due to insecurity in yourself. When fear arises, it does not necessarily mean to dive in, although at times it is required to overcome it. Firstly, you need to understand if you have what it takes to dive in, or if you need to stop and get what you need to dive in.

Would you blindly and deliberately jump into a pit of pythons or deadly coral snakes of which you are afraid to overcome your fear of snakes? No. You would first want to get appropriate training to accomplish such a feat, for example, learning to become one with them. Would you encourage a young child to face her fear of the dark by walking through a lonely alley alone late at night? No. That would be foolishly dangerous.

The key to overcoming your fear is not to avoid it but to feel the intensity of it, and use it to your advantage by figuring out what fear is speaking to you. Then determine if you need to dive in or not. In this way, you are making fear your friend, not your foe. The message may be such that you need to get more prepared; let go; believe in yourself as you have what it takes; something isn't right which you need to investigate further; have courage and dive in despite your fear otherwise, you would miss out on something good; or danger ahead so do not proceed or do so cautiously.

Take a close look and decipher the message in your fear. As you understand what is behind your fear and what you can do about it, you would find that fear begins to dissipate. Use sound judgment. Then take appropriate actions to go through and beyond it, as you can only conquer fear in this way.

Do not let fear steal your chance of living your dream of a happy and dynamic life. You have the power in you to take control and not let the thought and feeling of fear control you. This is liberating.

37.

Convert Problems into Solutions

Life is such that one never escapes the experience of problems. It is a means to become resilient, as it forces you to reach within yourself, to access a creative power to go through the difficult times and come out a better person than you can ever imagine yourself to be. Isn't it encouraging to know that we have direct access to such a superb and phenomenal capability as it exists in us?

When you talk about your problems, initially it is acceptable to do so as a means to vent your frustration. It allows you to expel some pent-up negative energy out of your system to make room for some clarity. It, howcvcr, is of paramount importance that when you talk about your problems, you do so not to give them the energy to survive and magnify, but power for solutions.

If you were to talk about your problems over and over to anyone who would listen sympathetically, without the desire to go beyond them then, your problems remain at the lower energy state of being a problem. As such, it is advisable to be very careful with whom you share your problems as some people will not be capable of helping you to solve them. They do not have what it takes to meet you where you are and help pull you up, and some quietly want to see you stay down.

If you focus too much on the problem, it would appear to be bigger than it is, as whatever you focus on expands and grows. If you do so, you could also become physically, mentally, emotionally, financially and spiritually unhealthy. As such, it is wise to focus on the problem only to the extent of finding a solution by lifting your thoughts to a higher place from where the problems occurred. Then you will access the place and state of being where solutions reside.

As you access solutions keep close only those influences that will help you toward achieving them, not those that will perpetuate and add to the problem. When you find solutions, focus on implementing them, and gradually the problems will dissipate. In this, there is power to advance as you find yourself in an exciting and limitless world.

38.

Make This Day Yours

This day belongs to you. It is yours, and you get to determine what you make of it. The choice is yours to turn it into a fabulous day by viewing it from the mountaintop or allow it to be a wretched day by maintaining a pitiful viewpoint.

As you go about your day, notice if anyone triggers a negative emotion in and reaction out of you. If this happens, instead of going down in the pit of darkness where the viewpoint is confined and narrow causing you to get lost in the emotion, stand on the mountaintop where the perspective is an open view. It is from here you can have gratitude for the person or situation that allowed this negativity to surface, and come out of you.

Why be grateful? Because now you have the opportunity to fix it by realizing that your negative reaction is in you to resolve, no matter what they did or said to you. Now you are in a position to address any issue intelligently with a clear vision as you see everything as it is, without the dark cloud of emotion blocking your view. Then you can finally put the issue to rest and be at peace.

Likewise, if anyone is the instrument and stimulus to

bring out a positive emotion in and reaction out of you, give thanks to them for lighting up your life. Then reciprocate by doing the same for others; by being a positive trigger in theirs. It is often too easy to waste your time and energy and lose joy by fussing over the small things in life, over which you have no control, such as traffic slowing you down or someone taking too long in the grocery line. Who knows as maybe you are being saved from a more hazardous event due to the delay, or it is an opportunity to learn patience?

Do not give others and events control over your joy, which is up to you. Instead of becoming intense and uptight during your delay which does not change or make anything better but increases your blood pressure, listen to some music that you enjoy or visualize being near calm waters, as these can relax you. By the time you arrive where you are going, you would be more peaceful and energetic.

Make this day yours. You determine how you will allow others and events to affect you. Now relax and enjoy the view from the mountaintop, as life always looks and feels more spectacular from up there.

39.

Be Stubborn

Yes, that's right, be stubborn. There are too many gurus advising people to be flexible and to learn to say "yes" more often. There is a time when it is imperative for you to be stubborn and a time when you need to be flexible. Likewise, there is a time when to say "yes" and when to say "no" graciously. In each case, there must be a benefit to you. Otherwise, you would end up becoming very resentful, and in the process could lose everything you stand for.

Many people perceive stubbornness as a negative quality when it is commendable if applied appropriately, and one that reflects the strength of one's character. Have you ever noticed that those who ask of you to be flexible are the very people who are inflexible and stubborn, as they are not willing to flex toward you, but want you to flex toward them?

It is just food for thought not for you to use as an arsenal against them. It is meant to help you realize not to buy into everything you are learning but to question the validity, relevance, and appropriateness. It is meant to awaken you; to notice if you are flexing with the wrong people, at the wrong time, and in the wrong way.

I admire anyone who is stubborn when it means that they do not have to give up something important that resonates with them, feels right for them, and do not have to compromise their value-system to be won over and approved by others. In other words, they are willing to lose the unimportant and keep a clear conscience, which is worthier than what others have to offer them.

When flexing eats away at your soul and depreciates the quality of your life, it means that you are a people-pleaser, and are willing to compromise your integrity. You are much more than this and have the exceptional wisdom to know when to be stubborn without being grossly selfish, and when it is necessary to be flexible to promote harmony in oneself, with others, and in situations.

Remember that you are living with only one person twenty-four hours per day because wherever you go, there you are. As such, from today start being stubborn and flexible in the right way so that you can live with yourself peacefully and joyfully.

40.

Give Up Unnecessary Control

We live in an era where we are learning that there is no need to work hard to achieve what we want. If you expect to do little yet get a whole lot then, you have misunderstood this teaching. All that "not to work hard" means is to not suffer within, while working conscientiously and industriously to achieve or acquire something. To get that something, you must put in the time, effort and energy which are quite rewarding. The key is to let go of your tight control while you are doing so that you do not become miserable otherwise your work will feel hard.

There are spiritual teachers who teach their students the concept of "do nothing." This teaching is also gravely misunderstood. It is impossible to do nothing because the very act of doing nothing is something. It is called action in inaction. Even if you were to sit and do nothing to get something when it arrives it serves no purpose if you do not do something with it. All that the "do nothing" system means is to make an effortless effort. In other words, let go of the inner-striving and control while you make an outer effort.

If you observe life, you would notice that there is merit in giving up excessive control, so you do not stifle the birth of something you want. Too much and unwarranted control creates misery and confusion. It makes what you want to come into being, feel harder than it should. This type of control takes away the pleasure and joy of it coming to life. Likewise, if you are too controlling over others, eventually they will run far away from you, and you could lose out on joy and having good people around. Relax your hold and let them be themselves.

Do your part. Let go. Give up unnecessary control. Loosen your grip so that the creative, universal manifesting power can take over and breathe life into what you want in the same way it breathes life into you. This approach allows you to remain relaxed within. Then, any action taken feels less burdened, and the journey feels lighter and more pleasant. For what is the purpose of having anything or anyone without enjoying the journey? Have a blast.

41.

Keep Empowering Influences

All influences, good and bad, have immense power in them as they shape and mold you into who you are, whether or not you are aware of this. If you are not on guard, these can steal your soul and cheat you from living a joyful life, as they subtly penetrate your psyche telling you secrets that you unconsciously act out daily. If on guard, you will let in only those influences that bring peace and goodness into your life, as the secrets these reveal will set you free.

If you were to examine your life, you would notice that it reflects the strongest, most dominant and consistent influences you keep. From the way you speak, attitudes, activities in which you engage, state of being, conditions of living, and how you deport yourself and deal with situations.

If you are spiritually inclined, you would have divine influences, such as spiritual teachers, books, movies, and groups. If you are materially and financially prosperous, your dominant influence would be the same. If your strongest influence is negative, your life experience would be negative. If your strongest influence is one that invigorates growth, abundance, spiritual evolution, balance, and helping others then, your life would more likely reflect these.

If your life feels depleted in a particular area, notice the strong influence that is keeping you in a lack position. Chart out what you want your life to reflect, and start garnering support in terms of the dominant influences you want. From the company you keep, the videos you watch to the books you read and the places you go. Make a deliberate and conscious decision to keep competent and inspiring influences that will take you to a promising place within, and on the outside.

Replace energy suckers with energy generators. Keep dream makers and discard passion killers. Instead of jealous and limited statistic watchers, keep passionate, expansive and empowering believers. Get rid of time wasters and use your time wisely with time investors, as your time on earth is precious and limited.

42.

Be Humble

Humility is a magnetic and attractive quality in any person especially, when it exists in highly successful people in the material world, and amongst spiritual people. It means that there is little ego-identification with what they know and have accomplished, as they see these as gifts of grace. Sadly, this quality is poorly lacking in both groups of people as well as in the average human being in our world today.

There is a misconception among many that if they become humble, it reflects weakness. There is, in fact, an appealing gracefulness not a weakness in humility, as there is quiet confidence when you know something. Humility speaks volumes in silence as the humbler you are, the less you need to prove yourself continuously to others. You are therefore quite comfortable in your skin, in whatever you do, and wherever you are. It does not mean to be stubborn in your rightness, but to have recognition of your errors, for which you take responsibility to correct. This is a strength.

Humility is a state of being whereby one is non-judgmental, accepts that one does not know, knows what one knows without boasting, and has what one has without deliberate and pretentious display, but is grateful, feels blessed and lovingly shares.

When you are humble, it does not mean to hang your head low and let others take advantage of you. Humility is quite a compelling quality as it is graciousness with a quiet confidence that makes others pay attention, and draws them in due to your humble and simple ease within.

You are encouraged to become humble by understanding that Life is very fragile and whatever you have and gained, you can lose quicker than it took for you to get these to make you fall from grace. Be humble and gracious, and you will find that Life will bestow many blessings upon you.

43.

Do Not Try to Change People

Are you one of those people who are relentlessly trying to change others and are exhausted and frustrated that it is not happening? You have arrived at the right place. Especially, if you think that life would be a blissful experience if others and the world were to change to suit you.

People's nature is to want others to change not for the benefit of the one who needs to change, but for the one who is requesting or demanding the change. There is that unconscious notion that you will be happy if you can get people to be how you want them to be, do what you want them to do, how and when you want it.

There is an unrealistic expectation of others to change so that they can be like you. In other words, you want a clone of yourself. If you want a clone to be happy then, you should be happy already with yourself. Indeed, it is a very noble cause to want to help others transform, as it will make a big difference in their lives, create harmony among all, and make this world a better place.

To help others change without it diminishing your energy, you must already be transformed, so that your happiness is not reliant upon their transformation. Then there will be no need for you to force others to change but may instill change in them because of whom you have become. Everybody has the potential to change for the better, but unfortunately, not everybody is ready to do so.

As such, you must have the ability to decipher who is ready to be touched, so when you extend your hand down to them, you can pull them up and provide a safe place to infect and affect change in them. If you come down to their level and they are not ready to be pulled up, they could drag you down with their negativity.

As you go about your day, do not force and expect others to change yet not allowing them to take advantage of you. Change is up to the individual and will occur when they can recognize the merit it will bring them, and what they will lose if they don't. Just be happy and let your aura and wisdom be a magnet to draw change.

44.

Give to Add Dignity

There is this enchanting yet divine quality that exists in the human spirit that causes us to reach out to help a fellow human being when needed. A life worth living is one that gives and is of loving service to others. It makes life feel more meaningful while helping another. It shows an appreciation for your many blessings.

Whenever you reach out to give to another, the most loving and caring way to give is to add dignity to that life, and to allow your giving to add value, no matter the form of giving. When you help others maintain a level of self-respect, you become a blessing to them. When you are a blessing you do not manipulate, or treat them as, or turn them into beggars because you do not see yourself as the giver. Instead, you consider yourself to be a humble instrument of position to give because of the Creator's blessings in your life.

You, therefore, do not make them run after you to prove to you how much they want and need your help. As such, they do not waste time, exert energy and become frustrated unnecessarily. Then they are in a better position to infuse your gift of giving with joyful gratitude and fire; to turn it into a lucrative investment. Give sensibly and freely so neither you nor your receiver will feel more burdened. Then your giving will never be wasted.

There is an old saying that instead of giving a person a fish, it is better to teach them how to fish. It is one of the best ways to help a person become self-sufficient and maintain self-respect. As such give work, give opportunities; teach skill sets; give support, direction and the tools required to earn a viable income which most people want, and would appreciate.

The reality, however, is that not everybody can be taught how to fish, such as those who are terminally ill and dying. All they need from you is your time and kind, caring, and loving help to make them feel a bit more comfortable and comforted. There are others who do not want to learn how to fish as it requires too much effort, and there are those who would want you to give to them in the form of lending.

If you decide to give to these two groups of people, it is best not to have any expectations from them, so that you are free on the inside. If you lend, be prepared to never get it back despite a well-intended understanding between both of you, as circumstances could change. This wisdom will prevent unnecessary loss, aggravation, devastation, and a broken relationship.

Life offers different opportunities to give which come in many guises. There may be a homeless person who needs a safe place to call home or an orphaned child who needs love and support. You may have sick parents, siblings, children, relatives, friends, or neighbors who need comfort and help. There may be others who need money, resources, guidance, and your belief in them to help turn possibilities into a reality.

Someone may need a ride to their destination especially in winter, to make commuting a little easier. A friend may need a phone call to know that you care. Your child or spouse may need your undivided attention and contribution. Some may need a second, third or fourth chance. A young person who has gone astray may need to hear kind, loving and caring words of wisdom to teach them that there is another way.

Give hope by helping others responsibly and not just to fill your need to give. In this way, you become a humble instrument to give lovingly, and caringly. Make life worth living. Be a blessing to somebody today, no matter the size of your giving.

45.

Let Go of What No Longer Serves You

Why is it you keep holding on to something that is not serving you well? It may be a relationship that is going nowhere, useless material possessions, a stagnant job, or any such related issue. Notice how you are carrying this heavy load that is burdening and weighing you down, as you keep dragging it along. It is stealing your vigor and energy for life as it is suffocating you and, although you are alive you feel dead inside.

You may be holding on because you feel strangely comfortable and safe because it is what you know, which creates a fear of change. You may have created an identity with whatever you are holding on to, and fear that you will feel lost without it, or the person. You may even fear being perceived as a bad person if you were to let go, so you hold on by seeking approval and acceptance.

You may be holding on to something to honor somebody who has given it to you. You are concerned that you could hurt the person's feelings if you were to give it up thereby burdening yourself with unnecessary guilt. You may fear still needing it or the person in the future although this has not been serving you well for quite some time. So, uncertainty arises.

There may even be the fear of being judged by others if you were to let go, as the new may not work out. There is a fear of becoming vulnerable, of not knowing what will unfold, and how. While there is no guarantee in how the new turns out, how you perceive it and what you do with and make of it determine the outcome.

You are above all these fears. You know that holding on to anything that contaminates your present steals your future from you. As soon as you let go of the old, you are freeing up space to allow in the new. Now new people, things and opportunities to which you are aligned can enter into your life.

You deserve to feel alive and have an optimistic outlook as your future awaits you. It is never too late. Embrace this moment and start carving it to create your masterpiece called "My New Well-Lived Life."

46.

See the Blessings in the Valley

It is not uncommon for each of us to go through the valley of life not just once, but several times in one area or different areas of one's life. It is the place where you can feel destitute, hopeless, scared and often alone. Although it is a difficult place to be, it is one to be welcomed. It is a signal that you are being transformed. Your character is being shaped to prepare you to meet what awaits you on the mountaintop. Without preparation, you would not be qualified and capable of handling this.

If you are in the valley, it is because you have created an association with defeating thoughts based upon false beliefs that have created failures, and fears to cause a wilderness period whereby an aspect of your life feels barren. It is a valley because it is a place or position in which you resent being as you feel down and immobilized.

When you are in the valley, always remember that you are only passing through not setting up shop there. Many people get stuck there because they begin to feel sickly comfortable. They miss out on meeting their full potential because they are unwilling to stretch themselves which requires effort, risk-taking, and backbone to climb out of the valley.

To commence getting out of the valley, you are required to stop resisting being there. The inner-struggle keeps you tied to the valley, as you exert and waste energy with inner battles. Be gentle with yourself. Accept that you are there and do not like it, but also recognize that you do not have to stay. Face your fears otherwise, you will remain in the valley, and miss out on what lies ahead.

See the blessings of the valley, such as the lessons you have learned. Then you can draw on this knowledge to devise creative means to get out of the valley, as you develop new perspectives on failure, and convert losses into life lessons to realize gains. Focus on what you have. Make the most of it, and more will be added unto you.

Despite fears that arise, you are ready to climb out of the valley and ascend to the mountaintop, because you underwent the preparation, and now have the knowledge and skills needed to do so. As you climb, do not hesitate to get those who are stronger than you to help pull you up. If there is nobody, then it means you have the strength required to make your ascent.

In the process, remember you have been groomed for higher things, so reach out and help someone who is also in the valley of life and is ready to climb up. It will make the mount feel easier as that person could add value to what you are being called to do. It is a great blessing, as it will take both of you to the mountaintop that awaits your presence and contribution.

47.

Touch a Life Profoundly

To touch a life profoundly is one of the most fulfilling experiences; to know that you have made some measure of difference in another person's world. There is no need for fanfare or heroic deed as you can do this in some of the simplest ways.

I will now share one of those simple ways in a Thanksgiving Day communication with a former employee who became an invaluable friend. In return, my heart was filled with immense joy at his reply, as I learned that he felt supported by my presence during some difficult times. The following is an excerpt of what I wrote to him:

> Dear Ron, I will use this celebration as an opportunity to thank you for our [many] years of friendship as we celebrated each other's triumphs; encouraged each other through our failures and disappointments; instilled each other with faith and courage to rise up and follow our dreams and be as enthusiastic for the other's lucky breaks.
>
> When I hired you [many] years ago, it was

> because I saw the potential in you to learn, grow and succeed, but also because I saw in you the human spirit of humility, care for others, and a deeper understanding of life. I hired you because I believed then and now that you are a winner with that combination, and that if ever you forgot these, as they are your true nature, you will always find your way back home to them.
>
> Thank you for allowing me to share in your joys but also to be a friend through the challenging times. It is what friendship is about as it is easy to have friends in the good times, but so difficult to keep them in the tough times. May your life continue to be richly blessed in ways beyond your imagination, and may lucky breaks which I call graces keep flowing in..... Warmly, Sandra.

His reply was as follows:

> Your message is one that I will treasure for many years. It takes a lifetime to repair the damages done to a child. Along the journey, however, if we are lucky karma shows up in the form of a friend. Thank you for reminding me of the little light within me. The storm has been tough and long-lasting, but I am far stronger today because of your voice and wisdom.....Ron.

When you decide to touch someone's life, do so profoundly by providing a sanctuary. It is a safe and trusting place where the person feels supported, encouraged, inspired, and reminded of the goodness that lies within themselves so that they can rise up and out of their struggles with a brighter outlook.

Take the time to talk to them, to gain a better understanding of where they have been and what they are going through. Be compassionate and respectful of what they share in confidence with you during their times of struggle by not using it against them; to cause them to question your trustworthiness or make them feel betrayed. They will respect you, and the substance of who you are will remain untarnished which will draw great blessings into your life. Do not miss out on adding value to somebody's life today. It is quite a rewarding experience.

48.

Put Me First

That's right. Put yourself first. It is the most unselfish thing you can do. When you make you a priority to you by taking care of yourself and your inner condition, you will be more pleasant company and a more enthusiastic, and energetic giver. It reflects someone with a winning attitude.

If you do not make yourself a priority, you will end up becoming reliant on others to put you first, and then complain and become resentful when they don't. It robs you of joy and energy. If you cannot put you first then, do not expect others to do that which you cannot do for yourself.

You have it in you to make you first, as it is a commendable quality that reveals a person of wisdom and higher intelligence. When you put you first, the quality of your doing and giving is far superior and more effective than when you neglect your well-being.

It is a belittling quality in any person when you sit and wait for others to make you significant. Especially, if you have not communicated this to them, and they do not know that they are expected to do so and in a certain way that is pleasing to you. When you do this, you make yourself secondary and a victim. If you are secondary to you, then do not be upset when others count you as such.

Are you one of those people who behave like a victim waiting on others to call you to see if you are important to them, and in the process making yourself unhappy? I recommend that you do not wait any longer. Make that phone call because it is important to you. You will light up, and they may do the same. In the process, you will pull yourself out from a victim mentality to a positive mindset.

Be a victor as it is a winsome quality. Make yourself important to you. Start carving out some "me time." It would be worth it. Make you matter first, and then you will begin to experience a shift in your inner world whereby, there is no bitterness but lightness.

You are now in a better state of being to add value to other people's lives including your spouse, children, siblings, parents, relatives, friends, peers, employees, bosses, local and global community, which reflects in the quality of your doing and giving.

49.

Preserve Your Earning Power

In this modern world in the pursuit of your passion, it is very alluring to abandon many cares including your earning power to accomplish a dream. To accomplish a dream, however, some risks may have to be taken, which can easily threaten your earnings. When you are undertaking risks, it is advisable to be cautious and do so within your inner constitution, as not everybody has the tolerance to deal with losing one's standard of earnings, and the many forms of losses that usually accompany this.

The moment you lose earning power, your purchasing power lowers and becomes adversely affected, which results in an increase in stress and dependency upon others. While to some people this is fuel to propel them toward what they want, for many this alone can create suffering in you, which you can project unto others to destroy relationships as you lose your self-esteem, confidence, and patience.

In such a mental and emotional condition, you can quickly lose willpower and drive to continue pursuing the very thing that caused you to make a financial sacrifice. When your earnings and purchasing power become weakened, they restrict and constrict flow and breakthroughs. In the end, this can make your dream die. No dream can stay alive and take form with a broken spirit.

Make the decision today to keep your spirits alive, to make the choices that will allow you to enjoy life without being an unnecessary burden to others. Sometimes, this entails maintaining your earning power at the cost of your dreams, to preserve the relationships that matter. At other times, this entails putting off your dream while you devise creative means to afford it.

If you choose to take high risks, keep the conversation ongoing with those whose lives would be impacted including those from whom you need support, as not everybody would want to or can be there for you. They may be working diligently and within some safe parameters to maintain their earning and purchasing power and relationships, and are expecting the same from you.

Grasp this chance at your dreams and approach wisely so that joy would be your reward.

50.

Avoid Idleness

A meditation teacher once told his class that it is beneficial to keep their minds occupied. I couldn't understand why he said this as I thought it would create disturbance in their minds. After many years of observing life, I have come to understand the depth of what he shared and what he meant, which is to keep your attention centered and focused in a purposeful place at all times. When your attention is centered and focused, then you are fully absorbed in what you are doing. A quiet occurs within, as thoughts fade in the background, and you experience peace.

If you were to remain idle for too long without doing anything productive and meaningful, it leaves the door wide open for the mind to create havoc in your life. When you are idle, and the mind is untrained, you can easily wander into dark places where negative thinking takes over.

You can then become depressed, anxious, discouraged and hopeless; blame, complain, hate and develop anger; feel sad and extreme disappointment; and become judgmental about others, the world, and yourself. It is the door of opportunity that is left open for you to drift into your past where many regrets lie or wishing for the good times and things that you had then, and into a future that does not yet exist, as it steals the beauty and potential of the present moment away from you.

Life is short and precious. Breath is life and every breath wasted is a moment of your life lost, which can never return. So, from this moment onward, use every breath wisely so that you are living a meaningful and flavorful life. Make every moment count. Keep your attention centered, focused and engaged in a place that enhances your life experience and that of others, so that there is no room for prolonged idleness.

You are meant to make the most of every breath you take. Look at the bright side of life, and start grasping its beauty, goodness, potential, and preciousness, and make the most of it. Soon you would see how life looks brighter as no time is wasted wandering into dark places, and your life would feel worthwhile.

51.

Stand Tall

To understand where a problem lies, what caused it, and how it arose, often requires you to go to the level where the problem transpired. To find an optimum solution, however, you are required to go to a higher place from where it occurred, to a higher level of thinking. In other words, you will have to stoop down, but you must stand back up tall, without which you will not be able to solve the problem effectively.

I will now demonstrate this concept by referring to a workplace situation. There was an employee who continuously complained about other employees' work, which created an unhealthy work environment. In that employee's eyes nobody could ever do anything good enough, or right, and if they did, not for long. Eventually, the manager advised another employee to come down to the level of the complaining employee to address the problem in a confrontational manner. Luckily, the employee was wise enough not to use this approach, but a professional one to achieve a more amicable outcome.

The manager, unfortunately, had a reputation of going

down to the complainer's level, but often allowed himself to get pulled down by the complainer and entrapped at that level of thinking, which created a lot of stress and turmoil for himself. Hence, the manager became just like the complaining employee in spirit, and attitude. Such an approach did not successfully defuse the intense situation to create an inspiring workplace. Instead, the manager needed to implement the "stand tall" principle.

Whenever you stoop down, ensure that it is for you to gain an understanding of the complainer's point of view and the situation, and to reach down to pull the person up to your level of thinking. When you use this approach, you would more likely resolve the problem whereby you create an environment in which people are enthusiastic, productive, and co-operative as they strive to exist in harmony with each other.

So, if and whenever, you are in a position to mitigate a strained situation at home, at work, or in the community do not stoop too low. Stand tall as a person of character and substance, and be a beacon of light to others. Guide them to pull each other up which will inspire and encourage cohesiveness. Then energy will get directed in productive ways as people are working with a greater ease and joy toward achieving a common goal.

You are a competent person. So come forward and influence others by showing them how to stand tall, and all the good that could come out of it.

52.

Practice the Psychology of Subtle Suggestion

When I was much younger, I learned the concept of using the psychology of subtle suggestion. It is a type of persuasion to get an individual to do something opposite to what they do without being forceful or placing a demand upon them but through the power of a subtle suggestion. In this way, you can readily prevent or eliminate any unnecessary potential tension, which would accompany insistence. Time and life experiences have taught me that this is wisdom.

I have learned to apply the psychology of subtle suggestion in many situations to produce favorable results. When I failed to apply it where it was needed, I also reaped a corresponding result, which was negative.

People who are close to me know that I do not appreciate loud speaking. So, when a loud and hyper speaker tries to engage me in a conversation especially early in the morning, I would deliberately keep the tone of my voice low and calm, which causes the speaker to naturally tone down their voice. It is suggestive and masterful as I get what I want without aggravating the situation.

I have also experienced the opposite when I make a gesture or blatantly ask the speaker to speak softly, which results in them getting upset with me. Their negative reaction could be due to them perceiving my request as demanding and a form of control, instead of an invitation for a more pleasant conversation. In such an unhealthy mental condition, they are unaware of the opportunity to calm down their agitated spirit.

I also learned the wisdom behind using the principle of "kill" them with sweetness. It is a method that allows you to win over others and situations without animosity but with kindness, charm, and understanding. It, however, does not mean to let your guard down by compromising your principles in situations, such as abuse which requires not too much sweetness but a stern and more direct approach.

In practicing the art of sweetness, even though you do not get what you want, you would at least leave a lovely and memorable impression upon the person that could end up bringing value to you sometime in the future, if and whenever next you encounter and interact with each other.

Today is a good day to start using the power of subtle suggestion and the art of "kill" them with sweetness in the right circumstances, and you could end up being a winner. Do it because it is genuine and makes you feel good within. Then, you can never lose.

53.

Get Rid of the Idiot

It is time to get rid of the idiot in your life once and for all. Have you ever noticed that the same kind of idiot keeps showing up in your life? The one who annoys you? And you wonder, "Why me?" You make every effort to avoid, hide from and even confront the annoying idiot about his idiocy. And as soon as you think you got rid of one idiot, another one shows up, and then another, and another. Next thing you know you are surrounded by them.

Here comes the secret on how to get rid of that annoying idiot. Take a mirror and look straight ahead in the mirror. Now you are looking at the problem and the solution. I know that this is tough to hear, but the real idiot is not the annoying one but the one who is annoyed. In other words, stop looking out and start looking in.

It is essential to look at yourself to understand why it is you are drawing such people or even situations into your experience. You will start figuring this out when you no longer have the intense desire for the external idiot to stop being so annoying. Then, you are in a space within whereby you can now bravely shift your attention to yourself to honestly examine elements, such as your emotions, thought patterns, behaviors, attitudes, reactions, and choices.

When you learn how to deal with the idiot in a way such that you do not get drawn into their annoying world, and you learn what you need to change about yourself, and what you need to do and do it, you may find that the idiot or situation disappears. Even though they were to hang around, you will not be perturbed. It does not mean that you must condone people who are abusive or disrespectful toward you.

You may find that Life will always keep bringing an idiot your way, to keep you alert of yourself, and not become complacent and fall back into old ways and patterns of thinking, and behaviors. You are a wise and brave person. Keep looking in the mirror, so it keeps reflecting wisdom to you.

54.

Create an Inspiring Environment

Every day you carry with you three closest companions that make up your environment, that is, your physical space, thoughts, and influences. All of them work intimately with each other as your thoughts determine what your physical space looks like and where you spend time, and the type of influences you allow in. Likewise, your physical space and influences determine the type of thoughts you have.

To live a life full of joy, peace, beauty, and possibilities start taking a closer look at your three companions and see if these are fostering what you want. Everything that surrounds and bombards you affect your psyche, as they subtly embed impressions upon your consciousness. These include the pictures on your wall; writings that are around you; the shows you watch; the news you read; the pitch of the sounds and music to which you listen; the people with whom you associate; the type of conversations in which you engage; and the places you visit. They are the main reason for who you are, where you are, how you feel, your attitude, what you do, and why you do it.

Treat yourself to an amazing and fantastic life by shaping

up your internal and external environment. Spend time with positive, open, spiritual, peaceful, loving, productive, and intelligent people to keep your thoughts elevated; and avoid negative, insecure, loud and aggressive people as you will become agitated like them. Watch shows that heal and soothe as they help you to unwind, and avoid violent ones as they create violent thoughts in you.

Read inspirational material that educates and encourages you. Display positive words and writings around you as they seep through your consciousness and leave an imprint that subtly uplifts you, instead of harsh words that cause you to become negative. Hang sacred and scenic pictures on your walls at home and in your workspace, as they will help to release stress and remind you of a higher power that is in control.

Spend time in nature as it brings calm to your inner being. Listen to spiritual music that brings peace. Also, listen to music that makes you feel happy. One of my favorites is "I Can See Clearly Now," version by Jimmy Cliff (original by Johnny Nash), as it makes me feel alive, hopeful and joyful. Enjoy life and be happy.

55.

Develop the Art of Listening

Have you ever noticed that when you listen to someone speak you are listening to your thoughts simultaneously, and you cannot wait to respond? If you can admit this, then you can become an attentive listener by developing the art of listening where real understanding occurs. This is not dependent upon you being the last person in the room to speak but on the space within from where you listen.

As the last person to speak, while being verbally quiet, you may give the impression to others that what they are saying matter. It, however, does not mean that you heard and understood the person very clearly. To listen attentively is to do so without incessant thinking filled with predetermined biases. Then you will find that there are genuine understanding and compassion without an opinionated mind filled with conditioned ways of thinking, and prejudices.

Most people, including those who wait to speak last in the room, listen to what others have to say, but with their ongoing mental noise in the background filled with their already programmed ideas, concepts, resistances, and even fears. As such, they do not hear and fully understand what is said.

To make a relevant contribution that is fresh, listening must occur when there is no identification with your thoughts, as they fade in the background, and your mind becomes quiet. Now you are completely focused and can give full attention as you listen.

When you are focused, you are fully present and this tells the speaker that what they are saying is noteworthy. You make them feel that they matter. It is from here there is room for understanding and harmonious communication. This environment facilitates a response from you that conveys to the speaker that you have truly heard them as you ask relevant questions, consider their ideas or even incorporate them.

I encourage you to commit practicing the art of listening with your spouse, a parent, a sibling, a friend, or your child by giving them the opportunity to speak ahead of you and be attentive and see what magic occurs in your communication, contribution, and solutions. Then extend this into the workplace environment and in all other situations, and experience the immense difference it makes.

56.

Beware of Transition

There may come a time when you make the deliberate decision to go to a transitory place as a short-term measure to help you move on to where you want to go eventually. In other words, it is meant to provide you with a buffer in the interim stage of ultimately reaching a particular goal.

Many accomplished individuals in the entertainment industry have taken pitstops working in positions below their potential, such as part-time bouncers and bartenders to support their basic needs while in pursuit of their dream. Such pitstops can be quite useful, but you must be very careful that they do not end up being harmful, such as when your pitstop lasts longer than hoped or even becomes permanent.

When you are operating at a level lower than your abilities and capabilities, you can get drawn into low-level issues that suck your life-force. This can eventually drain your energy to cause you to forget where you originally planned on going. When this happens, it is an indication that you are lost and entangled in issues that require you to transform, but you haven't as yet done so in the way needed for you to move ahead. You may even create an identity in your unrealized potential to define you as who you are when you still have to learn how to be humble where you are. As such, you would find that Life throws you unexpected events that prevent you from getting ahead.

Usually, when this happens, it does not mean to lose courage and to give up. It just means that your transition is a holding place. It is where you have unfinished business, such as something to give of yourself or even learn before you can move on. Your difficulties will make the prize at the end seem sweeter, and you will be more appreciative of it on its attainment, and not take it for granted which could happen when getting it too easy.

If you are in a transitory place longer than planned, it is serving a purpose other than the one you intended. Stay open to learning from it; to grow through and out of the transitory place, which was meant not to be permanent but only temporary.

Life will use you and grow you up wherever you are. It could happen in a tiny house where space is tight and limited, or a big house where it is spacious and comfortable; in the boardroom where you are using your skills, or in a job below your potential that is unrewarding; in a high paying position, or a low paying one. It can even happen in your place of worship or on the streets. Decide where you prefer, and make a shift if needed.

If you are not where you want to be, remind yourself that you are better than where you are. Get energized to realize your potential. It is within your reach. Never forget where you want to go. Keep your eyes on the goal as well as on the journey. Enjoy the sights along the way to make the journey worth it. Stay open to transform; to meet your goal gratefully and joyfully. You can do it.

57.

Take a Break from Acquired Knowledge

We live and function in a world, in which we are continuously bombarded with a seemingly unending sea of information just by the click of one's fingers, and the touch of a button. A great deal of this information is well-intended as it is meant to provide a way to do, acquire and achieve something, and sometimes sadly and dangerously how to be somebody. Often, this information is meant to help improve the quality of one's life experiences. When you do not possess the skills needed in a particular area of life, then acquired knowledge from reliable sources is quite useful, such as if you want to become a doctor or engineer, build a business, or even become awakened.

While easy access to information through technology has proven to be priceless, it can also leave you very overwhelmed and confused as each person claims that their way is the way. In other words, they are an authority over you. It is how you can get what you want and want to be. When information overload occurs, this can be an indicator that you have become addicted to acquiring knowledge. In which case, you can become dull, frozen and unable to make significant headway in life as you lose the ability to make your own decisions. It can even divert you away from where you dream of being, which can be detrimental to you.

If there are so many different ways to achieve or succeed at something, then you need to figure out what is right for you without compromising your soul. So, take a break from all the acquired knowledge you have accumulated from cyberspace and other people's mental space. Go into your inner space, where you have been ordained with a superb power with which you were born, to figure out and realize knowledge for yourself. It is where you will discover truth or falseness in what others are sharing as it relates to your life. It is where you will discover which path feels right for you as it resonates with you. This wisdom relates to both the material and spiritual worlds.

Become an authority over your life so you can access inner knowledge and determine which acquired knowledge is useful, and discard which is not. Do not underestimate the power you have in you as it is from here creativity, new ideas and ways surface to elevate your life.

58.

Stop! Take a Break

Right now, do you feel as though you are drowning? Cannot breathe? Are you stressed, exhausted and feel stretched beyond all limits and that you are going to burst at the seams very soon? Are you feeling agitated and getting angry quickly? Do you feel like a horrible person and burdened? All of this is an indication that it is time to stop. Take a break before you break and break others, too.

When you are at such a breaking point and tired of challenges, it is best to stop for a while to refresh, recharge and re-energize. If you don't, Life has a way of getting your attention by forcing you to stop often through ill-fated means, such as illness, loss of job, shattered relationships, or even an accident. Do not allow life to come to this point. If it does, then Life is asking of you to give yourself some attention as you need and deserve a break to heal and rejuvenate within and to make some much-needed changes.

It is time to declutter your life from too much stuff and things going on. Stop running away from yourself by filling your time and life with too many activities and people, which cause you to get caught up in them, and lose a connectedness to yourself. Do not use your busyness as an excuse anymore not to stop. It will be worth it.

If you are feeling overwhelmed, take some time-out and walk in nature as it would help you to unwind. Use it as a time to hand over all your cares to a higher power. Your burdens would feel lifted. Your mind and spirit renewed. You would feel hopeful, have a clearer vision, ideas for a new direction, and different approaches. You would feel energized and like a lovely person once again.

Give yourself the gift of a well-needed break more regularly, as this is when you get to dream, ignite your imagination and creativity once again. You would also become more effective, efficient, pleasant and healthier inside and out. Take a good rest, get a good night's sleep, nourish your body with some healthy food and gentle exercise such as yoga, meditate, and enjoy some quiet downtime. As you do so, you would feel like a brand, new person ready to reassess what is important to you and face the world once again with a fresh viewpoint.

59.

Lighten Up and Smell the Roses

I consider one of my greatest blessings to be having grown up in the Caribbean. The reason is that I believe islanders have an astounding ability that despite what Life throws their way, they know how to lighten up, be easy-going, and have immense faith in God. They are generally friendly and seek out any opportunity to make a joke, enjoy a good one, or do both. They love having a good laugh regularly as it lights up their lives, releases stress and puts them in a better mood.

There is a misconception that islanders love to lie on the beach every day under a coconut tree and do nothing all day long. I can assure you that if this were the case, eventually a coconut will fall on their head to knock some sense into it. Within my experience, such an upbringing and lifestyle do not diminish their work-ethic. I believe it adds to the quality of their lives and the contribution they make to their families, workplace, and society.

I have come to appreciate the importance of drawing on such a background, as I chose to live in a much colder climate where the harsh winter months and the intensity of life can take a toll on one's mental well-being. The unique sense of humor and colorful expressions that are characteristic of the Caribbean people even in the midst of disaster, and their upbeat attitude that life goes on, are what keep me sane in an insane world.

Since I know the advantage of taking time to smell the roses as it does wonders to your inner being, I would like to recommend that you kick back and mellow out from the seriousness of life. Enjoy doing nothing. There is no need to feel guilty or uneasy. It is only the egoic mind that creates false self-importance in continuously pushing and doing.

Feel the bliss of this nothingness and bask in it as you deserve every moment of it. Practice doing this with your loved ones. Enjoy each other's essence and beingness. It would release stress which was robbing you and others of joy, as you project tension unto them.

I would now like to suggest you keep roses in your home to remind you to stop and smell the roses, to savor life. Make the decision today to enjoy life despite challenges, issues, and problems because being unhappy does not solve but magnifies them. Lighten up and enjoy each tiny moment, without which what is the value of Life?

60.

Know That Life is All About You

Yes indeed, life is all about you. It is the reason you are here on earth. It is your experience. When you begin to realize the truth in this fact you would start to view life very differently and bring a lot more attention in on yourself. Then, you would begin to transform, and the quality of the Me that emerges is far more expansive and all-inclusive, which makes life all about you unselfish. Only then can you flow healthily from Me to We.

Realize that the external impacts the internal and therefore affects you. How this impacts you and what happens within you is what you are giving out to others and how you deal with situations and events in your life. Since everything in your life experience affects you, Life is all about you.

Notice in the moments when you impart joy and compassion unto another and make somebody smile, how you feel inside. You feel happy and like a lovely soul. So, too, when you inflict anger, hate, animosity, resentment, and self-righteousness unto others, notice how you feel during these moments and after, and how much you are affected negatively. As such, how you affect others affects you.

When you start bringing this type of attention in, and you realize that you are the one being affected by your actions and reactions, which cause you to be joyful, hurt, or tense you would look at yourself differently and deal with people, situations, and events in a more illumined way.

The more you notice how you feel on the inside depending upon how you treat and deal with others, you would begin to make the conscious choice to touch lives in a kinder and more caring way because it makes you feel good inside. Although at times, you have to deal with others firmly and draw boundaries, if you do so without malice then you will maintain a clean internal environment.

This moment is a good starting point to realize that life is all about you and in the process, you will make it all about others, too. Stop being bitter toward others who treat you despitefully and you will not accumulate stress in your body. Instead, honor yourself and treat people with compassion and understanding, and you would feel light and free.

Always remember that life is all about you, so make a choice today to do something awe-inspiring for somebody and watch how your world simultaneously gets bright. Be happy. It is a much better state in which to be.

61.

Decipher the Messages in Your Emotions

This message wants you to become intensely aware of your emotions, to understand what they are saying about and to you. It is unfortunate that most people are unaware, and believe that their emotions—the negative ones—are justified, as they get lost in them. Unattended, these negative emotions perpetuate throughout a lifetime as you create an identity with them, and cannot disassociate from them to determine their true meaning, and what they are indicating to you.

Your emotions must survive to justify what is wrong with others and your world. Although your feelings are valid to you, they exist not to perpetuate but to investigate what is behind them; to be delivered from them and become free to enjoy life.

If you look at your emotions, you would realize that they are like indicators or messengers emitting or transmitting messages to you about you. The positive and joyful ones are there for you to enjoy and radiate out of you unto others and into the world; to illumine lives. The negative ones, such as regret, anger, and resentment are there not for you to explode unto others but are telling you that something is out of alignment in you. Somebody or an event is triggering the negative emotions by pushing your buttons to bring them out. Do not mistakenly look outward at who or what is pushing the buttons, as your emotions are in you, not in them.

The people and events are merely instruments to bring out what needs healing in you. So, look at the one whose buttons people are pushing, which buttons, and why they are triggered. Then you can get to their root source and work on them to transcend them once and for all, instead of expending energy to get others to stop pushing those buttons. To resolve your negative emotions, this may also entail eliminating certain situations and people who cannot be trusted, are controlling, manipulating, and have an unhealthy influence upon you.

Decipher the messages in your emotions so you can transcend the negative ones and bask in the positive ones. Then you will not be a walking bomb that can explode at any time. When you attend to your emotions and state of being such that you become pleasant, people will not avoid you but naturally, gravitate toward you to enjoy your company.

62.

Peel Away Old Unhealthy Patterns

If you are anything like me, you are working on yourself continuously to be released from old unhealthy patterns of behaviors and emotions that work against you, to have inner freedom and live blissfully. These patterns of behaviors were formed unconsciously at deep levels, as you were unaware of how external factors and dominant influences from childhood to adulthood were creating them. As such, they ended up leaving deep impressions on the psyche, as they created layers of psychological imprints each time you reinforced the behavior during the many years of your existence.

Once you realize this fact about human nature then, you can start bringing a level of awareness on yourself to eliminate these unhealthy patterns and transform your life. This process requires continuous awareness. The reason for this is just when you think you have mastered and transcended a particular pattern of behavior, and you have started to feel comfortable enjoying a degree of freedom from it, Life has a way of sending you some external factor that could challenge this specific behavior. It could throw you off-balance as you thought you had transcended it. Your saving grace will be your ability to bring attention in on yourself.

There are various reasons why Life does this to you. Firstly, to prevent you from becoming complacent so you could be continuously attentive to your inner state. Secondly, to keep you humble so you do not judge other people's behaviors especially when they backslide. Thirdly, there are layers of impressions of the pattern in you that are deeply embedded, which you can only work upon in stages. A layer is peeled away as you transform through each challenge. Then, it is less painful to transcend the behavior, completely.

Be gentle with yourself when a layer surfaces and needs to be peeled away, as others will judge you because all they see is the return of the old version of the person with the old ways. Smile and be patient with yourself because you understand that it is just another layer that you are shedding, and this too shall pass. This is freedom itself.

63.

Just Be

Among some of the worst plagues that are currently infecting humankind is the inability to remain relaxed within oneself, as each person feels pressured to be somebody outstanding in the eyes of others, and even to themselves. They must measure up to the geniuses, and giants of this world. Otherwise, they are not desirable enough to be in their league. The average person, therefore, cannot just be. Neither can the geniuses and giants as they have to maintain their titles, which are accompanied by added pressure and demands placed upon themselves.

You know how to "just be" when you can live in this world and do what you are doing with your eyes turned inward on yourself. You are unconcerned about what others think about you, and whether or not, you are living up to their ideas and concepts.

You are living on your terms and within your inner constitution and vision, while acting responsibly; taking care of yourself and family, and helping others along the way. You can enjoy life because you have no fear of judgments from others, as you are not seeking their approval or acceptance. You are not seeking validation from them to be who you are, and to be happy. Thus, life becomes a more pleasant experience.

If you are nobody to the world yet know that you are somebody inside, you have found the key to unlocking the door to freedom within. Freedom to be who you are without definitions, conditions, titles, and labels. Freedom to "just be." In that there is peace.

Challenge yourself to go out into the world and "just be" without being deliberately offensive to others, and see how liberating this feels.

64.

Renew. Rebirth. Restore

You may have lost a lot along the way in life, but if you were to look around, I am sure you can find a lot that you have, such as the love you still have for and can feel from loved ones who have departed from this world. They may have left you with something that warms your heart today, comforts you, and encourages you. Although you have lost many things and people many times, understand that some things and people must go to make room for the new.

We will all hurt, cry, experience losses and failures along the way, but I know that once we keep hope alive in our hearts, we have a wondrous power in us that can lift us up to heal. It is from this healing an unbreakable strength in us emerges that allows us to believe again; to have the faith and courage to pull ourselves up; to press reboot; to start all over again with a renewed spirit. It is in this renewal we all have the opportunity to forge ahead and welcome a brilliant future while leaving those things of the past behind.

For each teardrop, you were relieving yourself of negativity. During your time of suffering and when you felt alone, it was a period of growth. When you were hurt it was for you to learn something new about love, and how to love completely, divinely and differently. When you lost, it was so that you can gain something new.

I believe that even in our darkest moment, we all have an unseen power within to start all over again, that lifts us and leads us all to our dreams. All it takes is to start with a belief and to let go of everybody's disbelief. I believe that love lies in every heart that leads us all to heal. This moment is the perfect one to start your renewal, rebirth, and restoration; to give your life another chance; to go on a new adventure. You have the power in you to do it. Just do it and light that spark in you.

65.

Insulate Not Isolate Yourself

To live the kind of life you want, one of the essential factors pertinent to achieving this is to be very diligent about those whom you keep as strong influences. As such, you must be very conscious about insulating your life. If you don't, it will cost you dearly. Then one day, down the road you will be asking yourself, "How did I end up here and like this, so far away from what I wanted for my life?"

It is necessary to insulate yourself because if you are in the company of those who are not well aligned with where you want to go, and their collective energy is stronger than yours, it will pull you down and away from where you want to be. As such, it is critical when you are transforming and evolving that you protect yourself from keeping company for an extended time with those from your past, who keep pulling you back to when you had a lower nature and tendency. Whenever you spend time with those who keep bringing you back to a past you wish to leave behind, you are wasting your time and energy.

While it is important to insulate yourself from those who can pull you down, do not mistake this to mean that you should isolate yourself from the world. Along the road of transformation, it is easy to do this because you often reach a point where it is difficult to be in the company of those from your past. If you isolate yourself from the world, it would be challenging to maintain momentum in the direction you want to go. Isolation can dull you and actually drain you and bring you down. So insulate but do not isolate.

Align yourself with those who have the wisdom to impassion you, uplift and guide you, and help keep you on track to get to where you want to be. It is, therefore, advisable to have a clear vision of what you want for your life. If you don't and you spend considerable time with people who appear to be in alignment with you in some ways but are out of alignment with what you want to achieve, and where and how you want to end up, you will get distracted and distant from what you ever imagined for your life.

You are stronger than those people. Believe in your worth and the creative power that can make all things possible including healing, changing one's ways, restoring one's life and purpose, bringing peace into one's soul, and turning blunders into phenomenal wonders.

66.

Don't Take Life for Granted

Appreciate life and celebrate it. It is fragile and can come to an abrupt end at any moment in time. There are many people right now, who are taking their last breath, which they cannot change. While you still have life, do not take anyone or anything for granted so you will not have to live with too many regrets. Look around and see your many blessings. Savor them. Be thankful for them. Live in such a way that it says you matter, your life matters, and others do.

Look at what is right in front of you, that you see every day and take for granted. It can be snatched away from you in the blink of an eye. Stop and notice it and make the most of it. You will not see a trailer filled with treasures of things, certificates of accomplishments, and money behind a hearse. Instead, you would see people who are there to say goodbye.

Do you take for granted those who matter the most to you? Are you spending quality time with them and honoring their presence, or are you too busy online and rushing around in activities? Do you tell and show them that you love and cherish them? When you are ill and facing a crisis, will you be asking for them, or your online friends whom you've never met in person?

Ask yourself who is happy because you are alive? Have you evolved? Have you given up on someone quickly because it would take too much effort, or you feared rejection? Did you give up a great job and people easily with whom you worked, thinking that you would always get ones like these? Did you lose yourself in chasing a dream and forgot your family and those who matter? Did you miss out on being there for them when they needed you most? Are you giving up on realizing your dreams too easily and quickly? Do you give more importance to your critics than to your happiness? Do not let them take this away from you. It is your life, and it is precious and priceless.

Today is the day to make a change and not take anyone or anything for granted. Start with a clean slate and leave all your regrets behind as you cannot undo what you did. All that you can do is take remedial action going forward and make changes that will allow you to savor life and touch others caringly.

If there is something you missed, go after it and get it if you have another chance at it. If you missed out on being there for loved ones, make a change and be there for them now. Do not just exist. Live to your last breath, and if somehow, you missed attaining any material or spiritual goals at the end, you can say that at least you know you gave it all that you got so you can have no regrets. Make how you live matter because you matter.

67.

Retreat from Battle

Rest assured that it is okay to take a retreat from battle. Give yourself permission as you do not have to keep fighting. When life feels like a battlefield rather than a playing field, it means that rest is needed. Otherwise, you would end up battling with yourself just when you think you are in a battle with others, and situations. Life then becomes suffering which means you have a strong ego-identity that makes you believe that fighting shows courage. On the contrary, strength is developed and gets charged and potent when you take a retreat. It is where new ideas, strategies, and perspectives come alive.

The best type of retreat is a spiritual one. It is a healing place you go to where you can retreat from the world as you know it, for a while. It is where wisdom is expounded and shared, to remind the soul what it already knows. In such an environment, the messages penetrate and embed deep levels of your consciousness that makes it easy, and more natural to spontaneously apply the wisdom learned while you engage in life's happenings. It is a place where you will feel inspired, as you meet like-minded people who want to live and function from a higher level of consciousness, and collectively that energy expands and becomes supportive.

So, do yourself and others a favor. Take a spiritual retreat as the environment is one where the energy vibrates at a frequency higher than your battlefield, because of its nature of activities to bring calm. In this way, you are in a better frame of mind to more effectively deal with others and challenges from a place of renewed strength, wisdom and inspiration.

Be kind to you. Love yourself enough to treat yourself to a spiritual retreat regularly, at least once per week. Then you can re-enter the battlefield enlightened and turn it into a playfield.

68.

Seek to Give Than to Receive

I have found from experience that the more I live from a phenomenal place of giving without expecting to receive something in return, the less needy I become, and the less empty I feel. It is a powerful place from which to live as you leave little room for disappointment. Likewise, the more I live from a place of "I want, I want, I want from others" the less joy I experience.

The more you place yourself in a needy position always wanting something from others to fill you up, and having huge expectations of them, the more powerless you are. Thus, the likelihood that you will end up creating misery for yourself and others when they fail to deliver, as nobody can sustain such giving. It does not mean that you cannot have expectations of others, such as respect, but if your happiness is dependent upon this, you will soon be disappointed and unhappy.

You have the innate power to seek to give than to receive. When you give you receive something more invaluable to what you gave. Such as no time to feel sorry for yourself; no room for darkness, but only pure joy because in giving you are affecting a life by building it up and adding some flavor and substance to it. When you are engaged in giving without expectation of return, your giving is not merely giving but filled with acts of loving. Then, you do not have the time or space to feel empty, lonely, depressed and anxious.

Liberate yourself from a continuous want position, and reach out and give instead. Be a blessing to others because when you are absorbed in giving, you are not seeking expectantly, as your giving fills you up. Do something nice for someone instead of waiting for them to do something for you. You will spark a flame in them that lights one in you, too.

If you have a habit of always waiting for your parents, siblings, spouse, and friends to be there for you, try being there for them and you would feel empowered, as you see the positive difference you make in their lives. Give a gift to someone to whom it will make a difference, instead of waiting to receive one, and you would hit a sweet spot inside of you. Life is sweet when you give, so give sweetly.

69.

Be Kind to the Elderly

I am dedicating this message especially to young people who are very much engaged in going after something, such as a passion or some ideal to build a life and to enjoy their life. I sincerely understand because I have been there, and I do not want you to lose touch with what is of true importance, so you do not have to live with unnecessary regret when one day it would be too late.

As you go out into the world to live your dreams and build your own family life, remember the love and sacrifice that your elderly caregivers, such as your parents, grandparents or older sibling made—not for you to feel burdened—but grateful. Be kind, considerate and patient with them as they were with you when you were a child. If they were not, then be to them what they couldn't be to you, so you do not become what you didn't like in them. It will one day melt their hearts. Bear in mind that they are not only parents but human beings with inner struggles just like you. So, forgive them where you believe they failed you.

Stay in touch with them as this will nurture their spirit and soul to cause them to bless your life. Make the time to spend with them and to let them know that you care by what you do for them, and how you lovingly do it, whether or not they were perfect parents. Help them to feel as though they are part of your life, and that they still matter by including them in your good times and bad times. They would feel needed and valued, not forgotten and useless. One day, you too, will become old and need tenderness, help, support, companionship, understanding, patience, and love from others especially your children.

I know it is not always easy to deal with the elderly when they are negative, unhappy, angry, complaining, and unappreciative. These qualities persist because they left them unattended when they were younger, which have become heightened in their old age. Learn from this experience. Do not let it deter you, but instead be compassionate toward their inner and outer suffering. Be there for them, as it is very insecure not to have others, especially loved ones to be there for you when you are old. Bring some joy into their world and make them laugh, too.

Be pleasant, positive, jovial, peaceful and a joy to be with while you are young so it is your nature as you grow old, which will encourage others to want to spend time with you, and not avoid your company. You have a beautiful heart and mind so use these to be kind to the elderly. You would be glad you did because as you grow old somebody may end up being kind to you.

70.

Learn from Each Generation

There is something almost utopic and magical that could occur if each generation were to stay open to learn from the other, to make this world a far better place than it is. It is difficult when a new generation comes into being for the old one to let go of what is familiar and comfortable; to embrace what the new brings. The evidence of this is visible as the previous generation thinks their music, the way they speak, how they do things and the way they dress is much better than the current one. Likewise, the new generation believes that everything they do is far more progressive and superior than the old.

The question is, "How does each generation maneuver their way through the insanity of life, crossing and combining generations to co-exist and create value for the collective?" To accomplish such a grand feat, you cannot discard the old blindly nor discount the ideas of the new too quickly. No generation wants to feel insignificant or irrelevant. One day, the new generation will become old, and they will also undergo the threat of insignificance. So, be respectful of each other.

This world can only evolve and become a far superior place when each generation learns to include each other's ideas, and not consider the old as washed up, or the new as inexperienced. Incorporate new ideas and ways of thinking from the new generation that can prove beneficial with methods that are relevant, timeless and irreplaceable from the older generations.

Learn from the mistakes of the old as well as from their wisdom, as they have much to offer given their long existence and experience. Learn from the new as they have fresh ways of thinking, and when infused with the wisdom of the old can produce an exciting, extraordinary and expansive blend of generations for harmonious living; to allow each to be relevant and significant.

I encourage each generation to spend time and talk with one another and enjoy each other's company, so you could learn from and embrace each other with open minds and hearts, as you tell each other stories.

71.

Honor Planet Earth

Honor this planet with its captivating nature because it is the place you call home, as it supports the house or apartment in which you live. Do not wait on scientific proof to verify if any of your actions can threaten your home. All you need to do is observe and live with a clear conscience. Naturally, you would be more considerate and conscious about how you treat Mother Nature and Planet Earth, your home. In this way, you would be more respectful of other life forms that exist and share planet earth with you as it is also their home, not only yours.

Look at what planet earth does for you, as she feeds your soul with the beauty of nature and the magic of a starry night; lifts your spirit with the chirping melody of birds, cools you with her soft and gentle breeze, and calms your inner being with the sound of rippling waters and rustling of leaves. She loves you so much that she not only uplifts you but supports your physical body and health by supplying you with natural food to eat, and clean air to breathe.

It is, therefore, in your best interest to treat her well;

to keep her calm, stable and strong. Beautify planet earth instead of littering her, as this is your home to enjoy, and of which to be proud. Every time Mother Nature affects our lives in the form of natural disasters, we need to consider if she is reacting to us; if it is the way she communicates. We need to ask ourselves, whether or not these disasters are messages that she is sending us, to alert us to pay attention to how we are living and treating our home and each other, and other life forms.

Unless we know how to honor planet earth as our home and be respectful of each other, we do not earn the right to explore another planet as a possible future home. If we do, all that will happen is that we will go there with the same level of thinking and destroy that planet and each other, too. All the resources used for such explorations could more wisely be allocated to improve lives and our way of living right here on earth, our home.

When you are busy with creating outer progress and enjoying the luxury of convenience, stop for a moment and investigate what kind of footprint you are leaving behind. Pay attention to how your contribution is impacting planet earth, your home, others, and hence, your evolution and freedom of your soul so you can take one step at a time to improve.

Listen to the messages of Mother Nature and take care of the home with which you are blessed. She may be yelling out to us to stop creating pain for her as we will end up incurring pain. All she wants to do is what she is meant to do, that is, offer a mother's nurturing love to thee.

72.

Bless Your Enemies

Do not waste time on your enemies and do not make others an enemy. Otherwise, you will become an enemy unto yourself. Be aware of them and what they can do to protect yourself from them but do not give them all your precious time and attention. If you do, they will steal your joy and bring you down. When enemies are working against you leave them alone, as they will eventually spin a web, that will entrap them. Do not get involved. Enjoy your life and stay focused on where you want to go, and continue being the best that you can be, and give your best to what you are doing.

There was a time when someone did something underhanded to work against me. At that time, I became very affected by what the person did. I was disappointed and hurt to the extent that I walked away from something that was important to me because I gave that person too much attention and power. Years later, I wrote a letter to the person expressing my pent-up feelings, as a means to purge myself of any stored up negative energy. I never mailed it.

Firstly, because I accepted responsibility for the choice

that I made to give up what I wanted to achieve, and no longer felt the need to blame that person. Secondly, I am not a hateful person, and because someone hurt me, it does not mean that I want to do the same to them by being revengeful. Thirdly, one never knows if one day that person or someone related to that person will play a pivotal role in the future of someone close to you, or you, or vice versa. As such, it is best not to dirty the waters if possible, even though you have severed ties.

I heard a monk advised his audience not to get back at their enemies as "Karma always gets the [fool]." In other words, you reap what you sow. There is a biblical teaching that says, "Bless those who curse you, and do good to them that hate you." I choose to pray for anyone who is against me so that they do not become a menace to themselves and others. So, my prayer is, "Bless those who are against me; may their ways be turned around; their hearts filled with love and their minds with understanding." In this way, I do not tarnish my inner being. I stay in peace, and I am free from their pull on me.

Why wish your enemy the worst when you could wish them the best so that they could become loving and caring people like you? I also believe that my Creator is my vindicator, which gives me courage when antagonism is directed toward me. Stay in peace.

73.

Forget Statistics

Many years ago, when I pursued further education, I got my first introduction to statistics in terms of how they relate to the likelihood of success, and failure. I had chosen my courses for the first semester and was immediately advised by my counselor that given the combination it was unlikely that I would pass all. I ignored the statistics as I was determined to succeed. I eliminated all distractions and came out to play when I accomplished my daily goals. I turned a deaf ear to the naysayers, stayed focused on studying and developed a studying strategy, which proved to be successful. I ended up getting A's in all courses that semester.

I have found it increasingly interesting how many people place importance and relevance on statistics to determine whether or not they would succeed. Such a belief was never fed into my psyche as a child. Instead, I was taught to pursue something in which I was interested, stay focused, put in the required work, and have complete faith in God.

In my experience, I have found that those who place a great deal of emphasis on statistics over the power of faith never pursue their dreams. They place limits on the creator's power which brought all existence into being, and hence, on themselves.

If you want to see your dream die quickly, tell it to the wrong person whose faith is in statistics rather than in you and the Creator. Anybody who tries to limit you, tell them that you do not accept it. You rebuke it and are sending their doubt back to them. So, go ahead and wholeheartedly and intelligently pursue something you want and already you are a success, no matter the end result. At least, you know you had the courage compared to the statistic believers to try.

You can be aware of the statistics but go forth in faith, confident that you have favor coming your way. You have an Almighty supporter that is all-powerful, capable, and far superior to the dream killers. Now watch your dream unfold with wonder, layer by layer, and step by step.

74.

Cherish the Small Moments

If you are one of those people who emphasizes big celebrations and achievements but not the small moments of each day and small victories along the way, then you are missing out on the best parts of life. All the little things counted every day can add up to much more than one big moment. So, could you imagine how much you are missing out?

I am one of those people who do not place a big emphasis on my birthday, which came with maturity and understanding. If anybody remembers it, I am in awe. If they forget it, I am not bothered and do not become unhappy because of it. I have come to appreciate that what matters most is not just one big commercial celebration on one day that lasts only a few hours in an entire year, but how people celebrate each other in the small moments every day of the year.

It is about counting the everyday gifts, such as thoughtfulness, respect, and helpfulness to one another; buying a treasure for the other in a unique shop spontaneously because it reminds you of the person; and spending quiet moments together as being far more priceless than one big gift of thoughtfulness on merely one day of the year.

In this busy world of ours, take the time to cherish your small accomplishments that lead to the big one, and share these with someone who means the world to you. It will make it far more thrilling. Do not miss out on the opportunity to be kind and considerate to your loved ones every day, which adds to and makes the big moment even more special. Know how to be with each other throughout the year, so that you can truly enjoy and treasure celebrating special occasions together. If not, you will dilute it to a commercial event.

Always remember that it is not just about the big day, but about the small days with their special moments every day that add up to last for a lifetime. Cherish the small moments and little things that lead to a big moment. You will find that you have a lot more to smile about and celebrate.

75.

Realize it is Never Just About the Thing You Want

It is an illusion to believe that what you want will bring you lasting happiness. The happiness you seek from the thing you want usually lasts only a fleeting moment on its attainment, a few hours, or a day, and sporadic moments throughout its existence. Pay attention. Notice that when you get what you want, it is the feeling behind it that you were seeking, not necessarily the thing itself. Now you can detach from what you want and enjoy the experience of the process to get it.

Generally, it is never just about the thing itself that you went after. All that the thing serves is a practical purpose in your life. It is actually about the lives, including yours, that you affected on the way to you getting the thing. How did you transform? Did you evolve in nature and tendencies? Did you become a kinder person, lovelier company, more compassionate and understanding? Did you become humble in the process? Did you help and encourage others or did you inflict pain and suffering unto them? Did you share what you learned with others through positive reinforcement? What kind of experience did you leave them with although you are not responsible for their happiness? Whose life was enhanced because you walked through it while headed toward the thing you wanted?

If the thing is your passion and what you are supposed to be doing or have, and it is the reason you believe that you are here on earth, but took precedence over the lives you touched including your own, it will not get you to heaven as you created hell in the process. Take some time and re-examine WHAT it is you are going after, understand WHY you are going after it, and HOW you are going about it, such as with care for others to ensure that you come through it as a less selfish, and a wiser and more considerate person.

As such, as you go after what you want, be conscious of the inherent characteristic trademark you leave behind. Be thoughtful and generous, and ensure that you create heaven on earth. Then the thing would be worth the effort.

76.

Use Negatives as Inspiration

I know it is tough to see anything negative as inspiration because it is much easier to complain than to create a shift in you. It took me a long time to figure this out, but I am only too glad to share it with you to help you along and save you from unnecessary prolonged suffering. It is a work-in-progress for me, and I am sure it will be for you, as you conquer one negative at a time. It is about taking the negative and let it ignite positive change for you.

When you see someone, who behaves in a way that you do not approve of, instead of getting upset, remind yourself that you do not want to become like them. If you notice a retired person wasting his life in front of a television instead of becoming judgmental, tell yourself that you would not do the same. You are made to do worthier things with your time. If you do not like where you live because it is an unhealthy environment instead of complaining, let it be motivation to carve out a plan of action to implement a change in residence.

If you are working in a toxic environment and cannot affect positive change there, let this be the incentive to find a new job, or open a business, or follow your calling rather than using your energy to get depressed and frustrated with yourself, and others at work. Start smiling inside and go to work beaming and with an upbeat attitude, as you are now aware that your negative work environment is being used as an instrument to transport you elsewhere.

When it is time to move on, and you do not, your world will shake up to help you do so. Before you move on, stay alert to what you have to learn about yourself in that situation. Yes, there is always something to learn. Welcome to the School of Life.

If you shift prematurely, wherever you go, that is where you will learn as similar experiences will arise. If, however, you are delayed where you are despite every effort you make to move out of the situation, it is because you still have some learning to do there. Be inspired. Use the negatives in your life to fuel positive change in you, and outside of you.

77.

Be Nice and Be Respectful

If ever you want to be a class act do not be too concerned about your stylish clothes or shoes you wear, the expensive car you drive, or the luxurious home in which you live. These are merely esthetics and are reflections of outer achievements. Instead, be respectful as it reflects your inner substance. To be respectful, it begins with you having respect for yourself. Only then can you be respectful to others, because what you are on the inside is what you bring wherever you show up.

When you have self-respect, you are more likely to receive respect in return. It is an indispensable and winning quality to any long-lasting and healthy relationship, as it determines how you allow others to treat you and how you treat others. Signs of respect are that you are polite, considerate, well-mannered and courteous; your speech does not include profanity and obscenity; you are not spiteful, and although you may be firm you are not malicious or condescending toward others.

In many relationships, especially between couples, when there is a disagreement between them there is a tendency to be disrespectful and revengeful, keep score, say mean and unkind things, and be inconsiderate to one another. In other words, they are not nice. They are, therefore, working against rather than with each other to build up the relationship. Their disrespect for each other will tear it down. As such, they need to stop and re-evaluate why they are in the relationship, what will make it healthy for it to have longevity, and what value they are bringing to add to it. This type of assessment is relevant in all relationships whether it is a couple, a family, a business, a friendship, or any other relationship.

If you cannot be respectful then why are you in a relationship with each other? Determine what you can do to make it a beautiful experience and work at it. Be nice. Be respectful. It says, "I am worthy of respect." Then, you will be a class act. When you are kind, thoughtful, and respectful to others, they will be motivated to help you and be nice back to you. Now is the perfect moment to invest your time in building up your relationship with those who matter, not spend it in tearing them down.

78.

Give Yourself Permission to Feel Lousy

There are many teachings in our New Age Spiritual world requiring further clarification. One of those teachings is "to give yourself permission to feel lousy." It is rare to find a person who is in bliss continuously. Most people have days when they feel as though they are on top of the world, and there are days when they feel lousy and down and out.

To be able to go beyond these negative feelings, you must acknowledge and accept that they exist. You do not have to suck it up. Give yourself permission to feel lousy. The misunderstanding around this concept is that people mistakenly believe that since their feelings are valid, it is acceptable for them to hurl their negative emotions at others, without their permission. If you are in a bad mood, it is unfair and offensive to take it out on others, especially if they did not contribute to it.

Everybody hurts at some time. So, hold on. Instead of taking it out on others, garner some compassionate support. Share how you feel with someone whom you trust to listen. It will help you to feel comforted, and relieved of the negative feeling. If you need further advice or insight into the problem that triggered your negative emotion, then ask for help from a qualified person. Try taking a stroll in nature as it would soothe you, or spend time alone to wallow in your pain, and as you go through it, you will be able to go beyond it when you bring awareness and understanding unto it.

The main reason for allowing yourself to feel lousy is to get rid of emotions that would otherwise get embedded in your being to create illness and deep bitterness in you if you were to suck it up. Release helps you to expel negativity instead of it accumulating in you. When you release, you are better equipped mentally and emotionally to do everything in your power to resolve the issue behind the feeling instead of taking it out on others. Cheer up. It is going to be a bright, sunshiny day as you make the changes needed.

79.

Do Not Develop False Entitlement

I often wonder if we are creating an ever-demanding society whereby people are developing a false sense of entitlement as we overextend ourselves to meet their expectations. The more you give and provide convenience, the more unappreciative they become, as they take it for granted; always expecting more. When they do not receive more for what they did not or will not give, they think unkindly toward you. They often become angry as they have a false sense of entitlement, and even give you a bad report.

Realize that you are not entitled to anything from anyone beyond what you have given. If you receive anything more, consider it a bonus and embrace it with a grateful heart. It is not an entitlement. If you have a false sense of entitlement, you are setting yourself up for disappointment, and inviting unhappiness in as a constant resident.

When you overextend yourself be very careful as you could also develop a false sense of entitlement, expecting others to be like you and do the same. You also expect something grand in return, such as greater recognition or payment without informing others of your expectation. If you continue going above and beyond and not receiving what you want, you will get worn out and tired on the inside. Then you will end up being very dissatisfied, resentful and angry. You will become a victim.

My upbringing was such that profanity was not a part of my language, so I expected the same of others while in my company, which to some people was a false entitlement. Not because I am respectful to others and worthy of it means that I must get it, because if others do not have this in them, they cannot give it to me. People can only give of themselves based on their capacity at a point in time.

I also had a false expectation of those who were married and had a family life to give me their time and attention. When I didn't get it as a single person, I ended up suffering. I have understood through life lessons that they created what they have, and if and when I am invited to share in it to be blissfully grateful, not entitled. This wisdom leaves me with a great sense of peace within.

An invaluable lesson for everyone is that if you are not willing to do what others have done to get what they have, do not have a false sense of entitlement to share in what they have. Get it yourself. Then you will not end up being resentful to others when they cannot, or do not want to offer you what they have. Realize that you are not entitled to anything from anyone.

Today, you are being called to be responsible, and use the gifts and talents with which you are blessed to help yourself. Do not underestimate what you can do as you are more than capable and able.

80.

Say "Please" and "Thank You" More Often

Some of my favorite words in the English vocabulary are, "Please" and "Thank You." I would also add "You are welcome." They are very courteous words that reflect a well-mannered person. Let me explain the power behind these simple words that are often viewed merely as etiquette but are much more. To discover their worth, pay attention to the words when you speak them. Say them not as though you are programmed to say them but say them with resounding truth in them. Say them because you mean them, and you would see the difference they make in how you feel, and how you affect others.

When you ASK somebody for something "PLEASE," you are first and foremost telling them that you value what they can give to you, and are not taking them for granted. You do not view yourself as entitled. Although you may ask assertively, you are doing so humbly and with gratitude, as the word "please" contains the vibration of being grateful for what you are hoping to get. It invites the giver to want to give joyfully to the person who is gratefully asking.

Whether or not you RECEIVE after you ask, when you say "THANK YOU" energetically from your heart, you are telling the person that you appreciate their time, effort and the fact that they listened, responded or paid attention to you. It keeps you grateful and in uplifted spirits, and you leave a memorable impression upon the person that will prompt them to want to give to you whenever next they are in a position to do so. The more you say "thank you," the more you are inviting what you want into your life, as it needs to arrive in that prepared place of appreciation.

I also love saying to others "YOU ARE WELCOME," as it means that I gave to them something they needed, which leaves me with a good feeling inside. It tells them that they matter. It also reflects that somebody took the time to say, "thank you," as they appreciate me and what they got. It shows that two souls are gleaming inside as their paths intertwined at a crossroad in life.

Raise your vibration by using the words, such as "Please," "Thank You," and "You are Welcome," more often with sincere intention, and see how your inner world shifts for the better. Also notice the impact these simple words can have on others, and how they react to you because you used the words meaningfully.

81.

Lay a Strong Foundation of Support

Building a high-quality foundation of support that is strong is a necessity, as life can be weary at times. This type of support system is what you will need to help carry you through the challenging times, without which life can feel more difficult than it needs to be. When building your foundation, bear in mind that it is not there for you to use as a continuous crutch to perpetuate weakness, but to help fortify you so that you could stand up strong once again.

If you become too reliant upon others and their well-intended support and power of influence in your life, they become your drug to sustain you, and you could quickly lose your instincts, intuition, and ability to find your own way. Then, you would soon realize that you drifted far away from yourself. If this happens, Life has a way to help you get back on track by making the foundation crack through change.

Change is the only constant factor to help facilitate progress. To survive it requires your ability to flex with it. When a change has to take place, it requires a degree of pressure, which when applied to the foundation creates cracks to shake it up and cause instability. The best of foundations built will eventually crack as they are made up of people, things, environment, and you. All of which, have strengths and weaknesses and will change over time.

So, if you have become too dependent on your support system and suddenly Life removes many of its elements and their influence, it is because you are being asked by Life to build a stronger foundation within yourself. Initially, the loss will be excruciatingly painful, but as you understand the purpose behind it, you will be able to accept it with wisdom, not resentment.

Each of us has the power within to find our way. Occasionally, we will need a nudge or a helping hand but not too much, otherwise, we would lose our sense of discovery; to find ourselves, to know who we are, and what we are here to do.

Without the crutch of influence, you can find your way back home to yourself where you can dive within to draw on your intuition, creative power, and direction from the Almighty, and you would find yourself much stronger than ever. That is something for which to be thankful. So, embrace change. Build a new and stronger foundation built by the works of wisdom.

82.

Remember How You Got to the Mountaintop

You have finally arrived on the mountaintop after much trials and tribulations, stretching and falling, and getting up and climbing again. Then like magic, a touch of grace reaches out and gives you that extra lift you need and pulls you up. You cannot believe that you are finally there. The climb has been a long one up, and you want to savor and bask in this moment you had dreamed about that is now a reality.

You have reached the mountaintop due to your exceptional skills, relentless effort from learning and growing, help from others, and a grace. Always remember grace. There is no value in reaching the mountaintop if it is just for your self-made glory, as you would quickly find yourself feeling very low, empty, lonely and unhappy. Honor everyone whom you met while you were in the valley—the good, bad and indifferent—as each one helped you either directly or indirectly, positively or negatively to get you to the top.

So many people reach the mountaintop and unhesitatingly forget the kind people whom they left behind in the valley; those who encouraged and gave them the strength to go on. If you are a mountaineer, you are relieved to reach the top finally. You got what you wanted. You, therefore, do not want to look down into the valley, as it is a reminder of where you have been, and the struggles you underwent.

It is advisable, however, to always remember what the power of grace gives, it can also take away. So, do not turn your back on those who were supportive of you in your valley days. When you arrive on the mountaintop and possess power, it is in your best interest to develop a spirit of benevolence. Recognize your accomplishment as a reward, and use it as a gift to extend a hand out into the valley; to help pull up someone whom you left behind. Your life would be richly blessed as you help change somebody's life for the better.

No good deed goes unrewarded according to the laws of creation. Just imagine how glorious it would be to have some delightful company with whom you could share and enjoy the view from on top. Challenge yourself to reach out and help somebody up, and life would feel more rewarding.

83.

Keep a Treasure Chest of Inspiring Quotes

I have found that quotations by sages, saints, scriptural texts, and people of wisdom can transport you to believable places of inspiration. These quotes encourage when you need a boost in energy to keep going. They provide a new perspective to see things differently, advice for direction, the inspiration to heal, reminders of the reward of transformation, and much more.

I hang several on the walls in my home including above my desk to keep me centered. In the past, I would often forget to read these quotes as I treated them as wall fixtures, but because they were so easily accessible, it also made it much easier for me to stop and read them when I needed some fuel for my spirit. I have now developed a habit of reading an inspirational or spiritual message as part of my ritual to start my day, as it puts me in the right space to stay focused on what is important to me.

One of my favorite reminders is a brief hand-written note from my dad many, many years ago when Life threw me an unexpected curveball. I had forgotten about this note over the years, which I kept securely stored in my scrapbook. I recently retrieved it and now keep it as my treasure close to me as he is no longer here with us on earth. His message is simple, but it keeps me warm, reminds me to stay focused, and makes me feel supported. I will now share an excerpt from it with you and hope that it touches you; to serve as a reminder of the importance of such a message:

> My Loving Daughter Sandra, I hope by now things have leveled off, and you are looking forward to a new horizon with ardent joy. You must achieve your goal. Strive for what you want. Have faith in God and yourself. Love you. God bless, Daddy.

If you have children, I encourage you to take the time to send them handwritten quotations or letters from your heart, as these can become treasures of inspiration for them down the road. As the quote or message comes personally from you to them in your handwriting, it adds a warm touch and will have a more profound impact in their lives. When you are not around, it may be the very thing they need to uplift them and keep them balanced and sane.

84.

Teach Your Children Well

There is a saying that if you are a parent when you are finished with your children the rest of the world has to live with them. So, teach them to be respectable, humble and caring human beings through example, as children unconsciously pattern their parents' behaviors and choices.

From birth to childhood to adulthood, you are creating adults of children. A child is impressionable so how you train up your child, and what they see you do and be is what stays with them as they become adults. It is what they unleash unto the world; the mark they leave on it. As such, when you communicate with them do not harm or yell at them to create disturbance, agitation and pain in them. Speak firmly to them when needed but lovingly so they could become loving people.

Cherish the time you have with your children amidst your busy schedule, so you do not have regrets as they grow up quickly, and with globalization, they could move away forever. When you are in their presence be there in mind, body, and spirit, so you do not miss out on their essence, smiles, adventures, and expressions. Take the time to listen to their concerns, wipe away their tears, provide them with comfort, guidance, and reassurance. Gather tools of wisdom and skill sets from resources, such as books, and professional and spiritual counseling to help you and them, especially during the puberty years. Parents and children do not come with handbooks. As such, be gentle with yourself as you do the best you can to be loving parents.

Encourage and teach your children to believe in themselves. Speak to them words of wisdom that inspire, heal, and generate interest, enthusiasm and vigor for life so that they grow into vibrant, confident and joyful beings. Guide them to deport themselves with dignity and grace as these are entrancing characteristics. Instill in them the power of faith through which they are capable of attaining worthy goals and which they can draw upon to help them through challenging times. By example, show them how to be kind, generous, and charitable toward others so that they become compassionate and gracious people. Help them to have a positive perspective on failure so they could rebound from it very quickly and move forward painlessly.

As much as you guide and motivate them to reach their outer potential and know their worth, lead them also to their inner potential so they could be at peace within and discover who they are beyond their roles, titles, and achievements. Never favor one over the other. By example, teach them to live in harmony with one another, and they would quicker strive to achieve this with others.

Always be their safe place to fall and assure them that home is home, so when they leave, they can feel comfortable in times of difficulty to return and be received with open and caring arms when needed. Teach them self-sufficiency. It will be an invaluable gift to them when you are no longer around to support them. Let them see how you value family and the importance of being supportive of one another, and they would likely do the same.

Light up when you are in their presence so they will light up when they are in yours. You will create healthier human beings out of them, and a healthier world for all. Celebrate your children.

85.

Talk to Each Other

I appreciate the fact that modern technology has offered us so many tools as a means for us to stay in touch with each other, especially when physical distance keeps us apart. Face time is a great tool to bridge this gap, and yet, it seems as though everybody is busy running after something, and having little or no time to make meaningful connections with one another. In some cases, people do not have time to send even a text message, and when they do, all they have time for is one letter words. The signal that this sends out is that you do not care.

If you are so busy such that this is all you have to offer, then you need to pause and determine what is keeping you so busy and why, if it causes you to sacrifice connecting with people who have nurtured you, been there for you, and who care for you. Is it more important than these people? It is time to go back to grassroots and learn to connect face-to-face, in-person, and talk to each other. Have a real, live conversation. Stop hiding behind messaging systems. Come out and reveal yourself to those who matter.

It seems that although there are many tools available

to make it easy for people to stay in touch with each other, many are increasingly out-of-touch and disconnected from one another. The reason for this is that only so much can be captioned in written words compared to the substance that comes through when you spend time in each other's company and have a one-on-one conversation with each other.

Face-to-face communication facilitates real listening and understanding, increases compassion through full conversations, and a better medium to learn about each other honestly. It is a means to develop trust as you feel each other's energy when you are in each other's physical presence, which tells the other that you care. You can feel the texture of each other's words and their vibration through the tone of voice, gestures and eye contact. All of which, are lost in messaging, as you are left to deduce what each other's words mean that could easily lead to unnecessary misunderstanding due to misinterpretation.

Commit to spending more time with people to whom you are close. Honor their presence by turning off your electronic devices especially during meals, as this says that they matter. Start spending quality time with each other and get to know one another more deeply, so you can have a greater appreciation of each other. It is how you can understand each other's concerns, fears, struggles, victories, dreams, aspirations, and in what way you can help.

Although you may grow and evolve at different rates and in different ways, you do not have to end up being divided or separated, because you are physically present and are experiencing the changes that are occurring in one another; providing support and understanding. Remember that one day you will grow old, and you will not want to have only your cold electronic device with you, but the warmth of the company that you took the time to nurture. Now is a good time to tell and show someone you care.

86.

Stop Blaming and Complaining

If you find yourself blaming and complaining and are unhappy because of it, let me give you some encouragement. You have the power to change this because all it does is rob you from the opportunity to live a vibrant life. The reason for this is that without realizing it, you are finding it much easier to blame others, situations, and events than to take responsibility. If you take a closer look, you will see that it is much more difficult to live without luster and vibrancy, as you hand over your power to live fully, to others and situations.

You are strong and capable and do not need to make others, situations and events become the unconscious excuse as to why your life is the way it is. If you keep on blaming and complaining you will remain in a weakened position of being bitter, and not be able to ascend to greater heights. Stop complaining about anything that you do not like and have no intention of changing, and over which you have no power to influence change. Instead, find an alternative solution to what you do not like so that it can work for you, and within your capacity.

Take back your power from those that do not deserve it and take responsibility for your life. As you do so, do not be surprised if you shift blame from others, situations and events to yourself. If this happens, you will end up tied to bitterness which means that you are still holding on to the excuse of blame, and the need to complain so you do not have to muster up the courage to change anything. It is not about shifting blame to yourself but taking responsibility to make a difference in your life and those who depend upon you, such as your spouse and children.

Here is the best way to go beyond blaming and complaining. It is quite simple. Stop it. Leave it. Let it go. Be kind to yourself and cut yourself loose from blame and anybody who facilitates and encourages it. What has happened is done so leave it behind. Let it go and do not drag it along with you in time. Unleash yourself from the mental noise that surrounds whatever it is you were dragging along. Instead, create the harmonious music of determination to create a "can do" attitude, and you will do.

Do not cheat yourself out of joyful living any longer. Let your music play inside and come alive so you can have much over which to rejoice.

87.

Behave Like What You Want to Become

There is an old adage that advises, "Dress for success." There is psychology behind this. As much as the inner affects the outer, the outer also affects the inner. If you want to present yourself as a confident person, you must feel it. As soon as you put on a classy looking outfit with stylish shoes, you would begin to feel confident and like a success, and project this out of you. Likewise, when you wear modest clothes, you start to feel unpretentious. Your outer garb causes you to start to think and feel differently. So, whatever you wish to become, start acting it out, and you would begin to feel like it and draw it into your world.

When I was a child, I used to pretend that I was a teacher. I remember my mum made me skirts to wear to act the part. I would stand in front of the neighbor's steps visualizing children sitting there while I was enthusiastically teaching them. So, I felt and acted out what I wanted to become. I didn't realize at that tender age what I was doing. As it turned out, my first job was a High School Teacher, which was quite rewarding and one that I enjoyed immensely.

I also had a dream of one day writing a book. I can recollect very vividly that while I was attending high school, I would sit alone outside and passionately write short stories and poetry, which just flowed out of me effortlessly. Again, at that time, I didn't understand that what I was doing was acting out what I would like to become by infusing it with a passion. To date, I have authored two books, which serve to teach, encourage, inspire and help others through this journey called Life.

I am not advising you to fake it until you make it, because if your self-worth depends on your outer eventually, you could end up feeling like a failure. To "fake it" is to be phony and the truth will reveal itself in due course. It is more about behaving like the person you want to become by changing the way you think and feel, which makes you believe it and makes you believable.

Proceed to smile, and you would start to feel happier. Behave confident, not egotistical, and you would begin to feel confident. The more you do it, the more you would become it.

88.

Bring Out the Best in Others

Life would be much better if we were to strive to bring out the best in each other, as there is much to gain; whether it is at home or work, with family, friends, neighbors, strangers, employees, or peers. In just about every aspect of your life, and almost everything you have to accomplish entail interacting with others, which requires your energy, effort, time and attention.

So, why not make it a pleasant and productive experience by bringing out the best in each other, while engaged? Less energy would be used to get more done. In comparison to when you exert and expend energy wastefully, such as in criticizing to condemn, blaming, and grinding others down just so that you could stand out above them, which is a reflection of one's inferiority complex. All this accomplishes, is a sabotage of the relationship and a setup for failure, useless consumption of energy, loss of motivation, and often stifling a hidden talent, beauty, or quality.

Every human being has both strengths and weaknesses. A successful relationship is based not merely on strengths but how you deal with weaknesses when they reveal themselves. Your ability to understand it, what is behind it, and a willingness to help the person go beyond it requires insight, intelligent communication, open-mindedness, and looking through a different lens. Some interviewers miss out on hiring excellent talent because they spend too much time on highlighting an interviewee's weakness that they lose out on discovering the strengths hidden behind those weaknesses. These lost opportunities are also evident in different types of relationships.

Today is a new day when you will look at others with wisdom and a fresh view. You will begin to notice signs of their hidden gifts, and a quality that can prove to be an asset. You will activate a great potential in them, as you help them to see that they are far better than their weaknesses from which they can rise above, because you see their hidden strengths. You will encourage others in their goodness, and witness an uplifting change in their demeanor. Have you ever noticed how people's nature change as they are reminded of all the good in them, which causes them to want to be and do good?

If you know someone who has fallen off the track, instead of beating them down, remind them of the good that lies in their soul. By doing your best to bring out the best in others, you are opening the door to allow in harmony, trust, and a co-operative spirit and environment. In the end, you will capitalize on the hidden treasure in others to add exponential value to the relationship. They will end up feeling inspired, and so will you.

89.

Grow Thick Skin

It is a great idea to grow a thick skin so that you do not get upset by people's negative comments, insults, and criticisms, but instead to allow them to slide like water off a duck's back. I, however, do not recommend that you let the skin grow too thick to prevent you from listening to and considering people's legitimate concerns. If your skin is too thick, you will become too closed off to learning, and you risk becoming very self-centered. The reason for growing thick skin is so that you do not become offended and lost in emotions that can prevent you from responding, and behaving rationally.

If for any reason you feel you are unfairly targeted in a mean and negative way by those who are against you, that is, your opponents the best approach is to stop yourself from responding immediately, if possible. Otherwise, you will bring yourself down to the low level of your opponent's behavior. Listen objectively. Empathize to understand their point of view as they may have a good point. If emotions arise in you to make you furious, dis-identify from them, so you do not become reactive.

Keep in mind that it is just your opponents' perspective. Take a deep breath and then breathe gently. Examine everything that is said, weigh it, and if you must respond then do so from a clear mind, and in a rational way.

Always ensure that whenever you respond to your opponents do so to further your goal. If you react impulsively, and negatively to your opponents you could end up in a tug of war and give them ammunition to use against you, and you will become distracted from your goal. As such, you could end up failing, and this would give your opponents immense satisfaction that makes them feel they have won.

Grow thick skin so that you can become strong emotionally—not mean and insensitive—while staying focused on your goal. Then you can respond gracefully yet firmly, intelligently, and assertively to resolve any issues, which can even win over those who are against you. You could likely end up in a win-win situation depending upon the mindset of your opponents. Whether or not you win over your opponents, your greater achievement will be that you carried yourself with dignity and finesse to command respect while furthering your goal or mission.

90.

Make Informed Decisions

I am sure like most people you would like the secret to making a decision or choice that would produce a flawless, and highly favorable pre-determined result. To make a decision that promises an outcome that you can live with might be easy. To live with an unfavorable outcome is much more challenging. I have been there many times and understand how difficult this can be, as you can live with deep regret when things do not turn out the way you hoped.

When you are in a dilemma as to what is the most appropriate decision to make, it is best to apply a process of conscious decision-making. Although conscious decision-making does not guarantee a favorable outcome, as you can encounter many hiccups along the road, it can be a means to help you get prepared to deal with any result. It entails applying a blend of rationale, intuition, and faith with the following basic criteria as outlined below.

- List all the facts that are available. When you write these down, you can see them with clearer vision.
- Seek expert advice from those who are qualified and whom you trust. They can provide more objective

opinions, guidance, and wisdom that you can consider. Caveat: ensure that they are seeking your best interest and are not merely dreamers or dream-killers.

- Include those who would be directly affected by your decision, if possible as they would feel that their lives are important to you. They may also provide information pertinent to your final decision that you would not have otherwise considered. Whatever the outcome, they would more likely be empathetic and supportive of you.
- Analyze the facts carefully. Make a list of possible outcomes, their cost/benefits, and how they will impact you and others concerned.
- Apply intuition but do not confuse emotions for intuition to sway your decision, as it could end up being misleading. With intuition, it feels right in the core of your being as it resonates with you. You feel at peace.
- Make your decision. Be fully aware of your inner constitution to be able to live with not only a favorable outcome but most importantly with an unfavorable one. Determine what the unfavorable outcome could be. Be clear on how you will deal with this to avoid being devastated.

Sometimes, in the end, despite your best analysis, consultations, use of intuition and facts, Life requires you to take a leap of faith depending upon the situation, without which nothing will change for you. If you do so, understand that whatever the outcome, everything will be just right according to the universal laws for your life experience. Make your decision. Then let it go, recognizing what you have control over, and what you do not. Trust that the outcome, favorable or unfavorable, will allow you to become more expansive and grow.

91.

Seek Counsel

I am a great believer in seeking counsel whenever you are experiencing a struggle in yourself, whether it is personal or professional, and whether it is from a capable mentor, spiritual and religious teacher, parent, sibling, psychologist, lawyer, wise friend, inspirational books, or a combination of these. It shows that you have recognized that you do not have the toolbox of skill sets and if you do, you need guidance and support to apply these to get through a challenge.

When you seek counsel, you will feel supported, less burdened and more hopeful, as though there is a light at the end of the tunnel. You will learn brilliant ideas, habits and strategies, and how to use these effectively. With counsel, you are likely to succeed but be advised that with too many advisors you could become confused and fail if each person says something that contradicts the other. As such, get a selective few who are proven specialists in their field, and always be careful with whom you share your struggles to ensure that it is with a trustworthy person.

I encourage women who are going through menopause

to be kind to yourself and considerate of others by seeking professional help to cope with hormonal changes that trigger hot flashes and mood swings, which can threaten your relationships at home, in the workplace, and with friendships. By seeking wise counsel, you are more likely to garner people's understanding and support, and you will solidify rather than ruin relationships. Likewise, I recommend to men to seek appropriate guidance to help you navigate your way through andropause and mid-age crisis. Then, you will be in an empowering position to preserve instead of jeopardizing your relationships, overall health, and well-being.

Whatever the nature of your difficulty—seek counsel—whether it is for business solutions, to heal a relationship, become physically healthier, overcome depression or anxiety, something spiritual in nature, financial advice, or any other kind of challenge. The only way out of something is to go through it, and what you do to come through it determines how you come out of it. When you seek counsel for direction and consistently implement what you learn, you are more likely to come out your difficulty wiser, stronger, more skilled, able and capable.

Be humble. Do not let your ego get in the way. Ask for help from those who are aligned with you and will not divert you away from the essence of your soul. Follow wise counsel by doing the work needed to live an enriched life.

92.

Start Your Day Powerfully

There is power in starting your day in such a way so that you give it a chance to turn out to be a great day. Morning has broken, and it is a new day, an opportunity for a new beginning. When and how you start your day can set the tone for the entire day. From my experience, the best way to start your day is to wake up early before sunrise, as there is a quiet and stillness in the atmosphere that promotes calm in your inner being to put you in an empowering state. It, however, may not always be possible to wake up early as is often the case for those who work shift. In which case, how you start your day becomes more important than at what time.

The first and foremost criteria for starting your day is to wake up early enough to give yourself ample time to do all that you need to do before you head out the door. In this way, you avoid rushing, becoming anxious and tired even before your day takes off. As soon as you wake up, start with gratitude for being alive and if you are married share a smile with your spouse. Declare out loudly that it is going to be a great day. These simple acts will give you an immediate boost in verve to face your day.

Stretch before getting out of bed as you would feel less stiff and more pliable. Negotiate with others with whom you live so that you can have some alone time to invest in quiet reflection, prayer and meditation to feed your soul, which will keep you focused and in a state of conscious awareness throughout your day.

Read literature that presents guidance, techniques, and reminders to help you deal with the challenges of your day more effectively and wisely. Also, read inspirational messages as they will calm your emotions, lift your spirits, and charge you with a bright outlook. Exercise or do yoga if possible, as it releases endorphins to fuel you with positivity, releases tension, and energizes you physically throughout the day. Partake in high-energy food and take the time to bless it before eating by being grateful and guilt-free so that it nourishes, heals and keeps your body healthy, and powers you up to embrace your day. Take a shower as it refreshes and rejuvenates you to enliven your day.

Now you are at an advantage point whereby you have the best of you to give, and your day is more likely to turn out to be a great day as you greet your spouse, children, associates, bosses, strangers, and the challenges of a noisy and busy world. Thus, you are less likely to get lost in stress. Start doing this every day and experience the energizing difference it makes in your life.

93.

End Your Day Peacefully

How you end your day, is equally important as to how you start the day. It determines the kind of sleep you will have and the frame of mind in which you awaken in the morning. In this ever-demanding world in which we live, many people struggle to have a peaceful night's sleep. To understand why this is happening to you and how you can change it, you need to take some time to observe how you are contributing to this problem.

The unconscious habits you have formed impact your sleep. Throughout the day, you are unconsciously absorbing different types and levels of energy that bombard you from sources, such as electronic devices, other people's thought waves, the news and shows you watch, the quality of interaction with others, and what you read. All of these, impact your thoughts, influence your choices and occupy a massive space in your consciousness to create unrest, and steal your vitality.

One way in which you can de-synthesize so you can sleep restfully is take a shower to clear out all negative energies that have penetrated your being. You will find that it relaxes you. Get yourself organized for the next day, such as write down your plan for the day, prep meals and lay out an outfit to wear as it will save time in the morning. The more prepared you are before going to bed, the less you have to pre-occupy your consciousness. Turn off electronic devices and stop watching television for at least one hour before bedtime to quieten down incessant thinking, which usually disrupts sleep.

If possible, resolve any issues you can during the day, so you do not put off for tomorrow what you can do today. When you do so, you will prevent them from getting lodged at a subconscious level to create disturbance in your sleep. Read something calming and inspirational, pray and meditate as these will help you to disassociate from any issues that you could not resolve to help you enjoy a quiet within before going to bed.

I used to love crocheting in the evening to help me unwind as I remembered watching how quiet my mum's disposition was while she was engaged in something creative. You can do something similar as it is relaxing and peaceful. If you can, walk in nature or sit outside and watch the stars and enjoy the quiet of the night, as it will de-stress you before sleep.

These practices will help quieten the mind as your attention is placed in a more calming space, to promote more peaceful and restful sleep. Then you are less likely to awaken agitated, anxious, or depressed and tired. What you feed your mind with will determine the kind of dreams you have, and the quality of sleep you enjoy. So, feed it with hope and peace, so you can have sweet dreams and wake up feeling lively and ready for a new day.

94.

Choose a Peaceful Path

There is a human tendency to want to be right all the time, as it validates who you are and gives you a sense of self-worth. It says that you have won and therefore, have not failed or lost. This need to be right can often put relationships at stake, offering it up to self-righteousness, and creating an environment to perpetuate arguments over active listening and understanding. The need to be right can, therefore, result in unhappiness and no room for growth through learning.

You may be in a situation right now whereby you are unsure how to handle. Ask yourself if it is more important to be right or happy, and to have peace in your life? If you are in a situation where you are always defending your need to be right, you will eventually lose passion and zeal as it steals your energy. If you continue along such a path, Life will show you how you are encouraging the festering of agitation, stress, venom and unnecessary worry.

I have learned that it is humbling not to have to defend my rightness unnecessarily so as to preserve peace. To do so, may require you to speak your truth quietly, clearly and firmly, and take any appropriate action needed in the situation but without fury and the expectation of being viewed as right. In this way, you can continue to give the best of yourself joyfully with less pressure on the inside.

If you are right, there is a higher power at play that will reveal this, if and when needed, and it usually requires you to let go of your self-righteousness. So, continue to give the best of yourself and give up the need to be right. Choose the path that fosters peace and harmony and one that does not steal your joy. Now you can have a greater eagerness for life and preserve your relationships.

95.

Overcome Worry

For many people, to overcome worry is easier said than done. When you are worried, the best course of action is to investigate its validity and what you can do to resolve it. Determine whether your worrying is based on reality or imagination. Unless you do so, you cannot begin to overcome it.

All worry is fear-based. If you were to look into your fears, you would see which one you can do something about, and which you cannot. The one truth to recognize is that worrying wastes time as it diminishes your ability to take constructive action and changes nothing. Then, worry becomes self-pity.

When you analyze your worry, and realize it is contingent upon a fear, such as people's perception of you, what they think of you, and will they approve of you, then it is a self-made worry. You are not responsible for other people's opinions. All you are responsible for is how you conduct yourself. Why should you become uneasy within for something over which you have no control? This type of worry is unnecessary, and as such, you can eliminate this in an instant by dis-identifying with the need to be significant to others. So, be relaxed, be yourself, and enjoy your life.

If you worry because you fear not passing an interview for your dream job, which will be a viable source of income to ensure you are self-supportive, this is not a worry. It is a legitimate concern, but there is something you can do that is in your control. As such, there is no need to worry. Do not focus on the possible outcome which is not a reality as yet. It is only imaginary. Instead, focus on what is real, which is to get as prepared as you possibly could to allow you to perform your best in the interview.

You responsibly addressed the problem by finding a solution to overcome worry. Now, relinquish your hold on the outcome, which is not in your hands. So, no need to worry. If you are meant to have this job, it will be yours. If not, trust that Life will lead you or bring you to what is for you. Have faith that you will be taken care of as long as you continue to do that which is in your control.

Love the gift of your life enough to overcome worry by directing your focus to find solutions for your problems, as these are real and in your control. Release all those things over which you have no control. Now you are free from worry and can breathe easier.

96.

Mind Your Own Business

Life is short with little time to do what you are here to fulfill, which is to learn, transform, and evolve as well as discover an individual physical expression that will facilitate these. If you spend your time in minding other people's business, you would not have much time left to take care of your business and enjoy life. My best advice to you is to avoid engagements with anyone who will encourage you into the world of minding other people's business, as these people have too much time on their hands, and are not using it productively. They have nothing better to do as they have no real, meaningful purpose in their lives.

You do not need to be sucked into other people's business unless you are there to help, provide incentive, offer guidance from a caring but detached place, and to learn from other people's mistakes. When you mind your own business, you shut the door on gossip, ill-speaking others, being judgmental and criticizing other people's choices, comparing yourself to others, getting entangled in a web of lies, hurt, unhappiness; losing out on opportunities, and most importantly wasting your precious time on useless issues that deter you from achieving your goals.

It is easy to get distracted by people's stuff, so you do not have to focus on yours. If you get entangled in minding other people's business, they will occupy a space in your mind that you need for creative thinking for your life. Mind your own business about your life, and you would find that you have no time left to mind other people's business.

It is a full-time job to look at oneself, your own life choices, achieving goals, creating a healthy family life, advancing in your career, improving your habits, learning and growing from your own mistakes, transforming, enjoying life, and evolving spiritually. Put first things first. Take care of your business and your family.

You are born for better and greater things. Mind your own business and direct your energy, time and attention to your life so you can live a more fulfilling, purposeful and productive one. Make your time on earth worth it. Dedicate it to your evolution.

97.

Surrender to Let Life Flow

Without surrender, you can get in the way of letting life flow. It is often the missing link to joy and peace in one's life, and to allowing something you want to come into being. Surrender is more of an inward action rather than an outward action. Hence, the challenge to surrender, as it requires you to stop the demands of, "I want what I want." "I want it my way and within my specified time."

Surrender does not mean to resign and give up, or not take action. It is an acceptance of life as it is in this very moment which delivers you from struggle and suffering, to allow life to flow. Accepting life as it is, does not mean that you have to stay in a situation or condition with which you are not enjoying. When you surrender, there is no inner fight as you are accepting this is the way it is, but you recognize that it is not pleasant and do not like it, and understand that it does not have to continue this way.

When you are no longer resisting, energy is not wasted but is now available for you to do what is necessary to change the situation or condition. When you stop resisting you are operating in a place of greater ease within, and this is when you start facilitating any shift that needs to occur.

When you surrender, you are doing so to a level of intelligence that is beyond your normal level of understanding. Surrender may not directly change the situation, but it transforms you. That transformed state is what allows a higher intelligence that is called God to take over, and it is the space in which what appears to be a miracle occurs, as you no longer block the flow of life and what you want.

Often it is when you are least concerned about having something that favor comes your way because you are relaxed and not stifling it. Give up the inner battle as you take intelligent action. Let that higher intelligence take over so you could be relaxed and at peace.

98.

Do Ordinary Things for Your Family with Extraordinary Love

I am very happy and grateful that my sister had the strength of character at the tender age of fifteen years old to be there for us, her three younger siblings, during a difficult period in our lives. It meant that she had no time to go through adolescence as she had to be mature, and guide us. She cooked our meals, prepared our lunches for school, helped us with our studies and homework, laundered our clothes and allocated chores. She also took us to church, made the Christmas celebrations and other occasions festive and enjoyable for us, wiped away our tears, addressed our concerns, made us feel safe, disciplined us so as to keep us on a straight path, and helped us to develop into responsible adults while setting the example of making the most of an education. My sister was our rock and happy place.

I know she made many sacrifices including going after a dream she had. Despite this, she was never bitter or resentful toward us. I am glad my sister chose us. She stayed committed to and was fully there for us. I cannot once remember ever hearing my sister complain that we were a burden or inconvenience to her even in the midst of my emotional outbursts as a child, for which I apologized to her when I became an adult, as I realized the extraordinary love she gave to us.

Whatever good quality exists in me, I attest this to her influence in my life, for which I am forever grateful. My sister has gained well-deserved respect, love, and appreciation from my brothers and me. During this period, I was also glad to have the warm, comforting company and closeness of my two brothers. I now have a deeper understanding of how important it is to help within one's family first.

Charity begins at home, as charity is love. Often, it is easier to give to the underprivileged, or help a stranger than your family. To support your family might entail greater sacrifice and inconvenience; plans may have to change; and things could be messy, complicated and challenging. All of which, could threaten your peace. It means there is no public heroism involved, or community, or worldwide recognition for your good deed but only pure love, care, concern, compassion and tested patience, which in my opinion is true heroism.

I now invite you to look within your own family and extended family and see to whom you can give something ordinary with extraordinary love that they need and want, and that you can provide to make it extraordinarily special for them. You could end up changing and making a big difference in somebody's life within your own family.

It could be as simple as cut down the time you spend online and use that time instead to connect face-to-face with a family member who needs you. Some of them may just need a phone call to check in on them regularly, so they know that family cares. Others may need another chance, a place to live and help to use their talents so they could help themselves.

Become qualified as a loving giver within your family circle, so that you could be qualified to give lovingly to your global family.

99.

Prepare for Old Age

When we are young, we all feel invincible and cannot even imagine that one day we would eventually get old. In our youth, we are excited about the future and what it holds for us, and we focus our energies on enjoying life and fulfilling dreams, as our now is of great concern.

While it is necessary to live in your now, so you do not miss out on joy and opportunities that are before you, it is vital to take into consideration how all your decisions and choices can have a long-term impact on your life when you become old. The best place to start preparing for old age is when you are young because, by the time you are old, it might more than likely be too late.

I present you only with some ideas and areas for consideration, upon which you can build and extend as is relevant to you. Your greatest wealth is your physical health. Make healthy food choices as part of your lifestyle and keep active. Be attentive to your muscle mass to maintain strength, and to your bone density which often becomes fragile and makes mobility more challenging when you get older. Ensure that you get enough sunshine and vitamin D to boost your immune system and mood. Practice postures as offered in yoga to maintain flexibility and balance, which become crucial as you age. Take care of your mental, emotional and spiritual health as a means to grow, evolve, and eliminate stress by engaging in prayer and meditation, seeking counsel, and filtering the environment in which you spend time, without which stress would leave a memory in your cells to create illness in the body.

Although you want to pursue dreams, always ensure that you live in physical proximity to loved ones, such as your family. As you age, you would value their support and nearness in times of distress, and you would not have regret because you can be there for them, too. Closeness of loved ones can add years to your life. If you live in a cold climate, consider how you could become confined as your tolerance for the cold weather decreases with age. If you prefer a warmer climate during the winter months, implement a plan to accommodate this.

In your youth, be wise about your money. Secure your finances, home, and transportation so you could be independent in your old age, and not be too reliant upon others and systems. The times in which we live are changing, and it may not be feasible to count on systems and too many people to support you. Pursue your dreams while you are young, but be wise about undertaking too many unmanageable high risks, because when you get old, it could be too late to make a difference in terms of providing security for yourself. Any insecurity will lead to a very stressful and unhappy life as you age. Be cautious about whom you allow to influence your choices so that you are not allured by their tempting offers and needs that could jeopardize your financial health and well-being.

Remember to enjoy life, be light-hearted and seek out peace, so this becomes your nature into old-age. If you put these ideas in place from young, it would be easier to sustain as it would feel normal for you by the time you grow old. You would be grateful that you did. Without the concerns or worry for the necessities of life, you are then in an empowering position to dedicate the rest of your life to the evolution of your consciousness, which is the purpose of your existence.

I suggest that you spend some time with a few old people and listen to what they have to share with you about aging, so you could learn from their triumphs, mistakes, and failures, as I have learned from my own.

100.

Slow Down

What is the hurry and where is it really taking you? Have you ever stopped to ask yourself these questions? At the dawn of technology, we expected that it would save us time, as it promised to provide efficiency. Life, however, has become busier and more fast-paced than ever before with most people having little time to enjoy it. Improved and advanced technology also promised to keep us connected yet, so many people are disconnected in themselves and with each other.

In our western society, it seems as though people are proud of how busy they always are. It gives them a false sense of importance. The more you become busy, more uptight you are. The more wound up you are, the faster you talk thereby, making it difficult to absorb everything you say; and the quicker you walk to give the impression that you are busy and assertive. Instead, what you are giving out is that you are intense. When you are wound up, there is a tendency to become impatient, aggressive, unpleasant, tiring to deal with, and tired. How can you feel good within yourself when you have such an impact on others, and effect on yourself?

With all the busyness of life, ask yourself some more questions. "How are you improving as a human being? Are you becoming a kinder, gentler, patient, caring, and sweeter person?" "Are you consistently enjoying life?" "Are you ignoring and missing out on the people and things that matter?" "Are you peaceful?" It is time to start slowing down a bit. Be kind to you so you could be kind to others.

Start talking slower as it would be a joy to listen to what you have to say. Start being less rushed when you are driving. It would be a safer and less tense experience for all. Start walking slower and look around and notice the gentleness of the soft breeze kissing your face, feel the earth under your feet and the peaceful feeling that comes over you.

Slow down and eat. Take your time to taste all the flavors in every bite so you could enjoy your food. You might even lose weight in the process as studies show that it allows sufficient time for the brain to register that you have eaten, which causes you to eat less. Stop and notice the smiles that light up your children's face as it would put a smile on yours and in your heart. Savor the beauty of a rose petal, its softness, and gentleness and take the time to marvel at the wonder of creation as it relaxes you. In these moments, tune in to the change in you, and how you feel more at ease.

When you slow down, you will start to feel less stressed, which could lead to you being much more efficient and effective due to how much calmer you are. Slow down to savor life. Otherwise, why be alive?

101.

Craft Your Eulogy

I may not be responsible for people's perceptions of me, but I am responsible for how I live my life, and if I decide that I want a eulogy what this should convey at my funeral. Many, many years ago when I attended my first Stephen Covey workshop, it included the topic, "Begin with the end in mind." Crafting a living eulogy is the same concept as it is a reference point to create a vision to help shape your life. It is an excellent source to keep you on course to achieve your goals, even though you will have to do ongoing edits as you change and mature.

Generally, at funerals, people highlight all the good aspects of a person but omit all the dark areas. A living eulogy can help you to look at ways to start correcting those dark areas of your life so as to leave a better legacy behind. I will now caution you not to try to make yourself sound like Superman or Wonder woman when you create your eulogy. Keep it real, honest, doable, and attainable but also factor in enough challenge to rise and meet a higher potential in you.

As you craft your living eulogy, ask yourself if you were

to be present at your funeral service, "What do I want to hear about me in terms of the quality of person I became? How was my character shaped through challenging times? Did I improve as an individual, a spouse, a parent, a child, a sibling, a friend and what was my contribution to them and society? Did I make a difference in somebody's life by seeking to give than to receive? Did I pursue a dream without ruining the relationships I treasure most, and if I did what did I do to correct this? Did I let the people whom I love know it and feel it? Did I become less selfish and a more caring, peaceful and joyful person? Did I forgive? Did I make a relentless effort in these areas even though at times I failed, and did I try again?"

Make every moment count. Start crafting your living eulogy as it can be an invaluable instrument to help you remember your aspirations, the things you want to do, the evolved person you want to become, and to discard what is no longer of value to you. No matter how old you are, it is never too late to take steps to make things right. It is better to have tried and lost than not to have tried at all.

102.

Define Success for Yourself

With so much information out there in the world as to what success means, it can be a very daunting task to become successful. As such, you can feel overwhelmed and pressured to achieve success as defined by others. To live a happy life, do not allow others to tell you what success is for you. You determine what this means to you, as it is different for each person. The route you take to achieve success could also be different. It all depends upon what you want, and with each person believing that their method is the best one, you can become very confused.

I have experienced both victories and failures. By paying attention to life, I have come to realize that there are some major underlying principles or elements required to come together to achieve what you want. Whenever these principles are not applied, one often experiences failure. To ensure that you do not set up yourself to fail, first and foremost, you have to stop living in the past by dropping all baggage. Stop blaming and complaining about what didn't work out; stop doing nothing to help yourself; eliminate all limiting beliefs that work against you, and pay no heed to those who are envious of you, and want to bring you down.

Begin by knowing exactly what you want, and why you want it so that you have a clear vision of it. Write it down to help define it. Do not keep changing your mind about what you want as it will lose power. Infuse it with belief, faith, and surrender, so you do not stifle it, and you. Now you are well-suited to make an effortless effort while you take consistent, committed, disciplined, and persistent actions to achieve your daily goals, which help to maintain momentum. Connect your daily goals to your vision, the bigger goal.

Always remember where you want to go but leave it alone. If you focus too much on the end, you will not direct sufficient attention to the steps you need to take to get where you want to go, and you will end up only dreaming. So, focus on the steps that lead to the end goal, as many distractions will come along to cause you to trip-up if you pay heed to them. If and when you get off-track, get back on track quickly, without which you could lose motivation to continue as it will take more effort to do so.

Keep the right influences in to amass support and guidance for what you want. Be flexible with your plans, goals, and visions as Life will often send you some unexpected events that require you to be flexible and adjust. Do not be too rigid about who should help you because Life has a way of sending you the least expected to provide support, and resources from surprising places. If you stay open, you will recognize and embrace them. Otherwise, you could remain stuck in waiting.

As these elements align, together with a touch of magic called grace, plus you enjoy what you are doing even though some aspects may not be pleasurable but challenging, you are well-positioned to succeed in due course. Life is what you make of it, so make it a joyous experience. Remember to count all your little successes along the way as they are equally relevant to the big one. Enjoy your exploits and adventures.

103.

Work with Love

In an ideal world, everybody will be doing the work that they dream of and love and would love doing. I doubt very much that in such a world, there would be maids, janitors, and garbage collectors. When you check into a hotel as a guest, you would receive cleaning supplies to clean your room, toilet, and bath because in that ideal world those who would otherwise be cleaners are jetting off to their dream jobs.

Not everybody would have a livelihood that is their dream job, the work they love doing. To support your family, you may be one of those people who have to be practical and responsible by taking a job other than your dream job. Your work may not be what you want to do but have to do. It may not be work that you love, but this does not mean that you cannot do it with love. Your workplace is where you spend most of your time. So, if you were to do your work that you do not love with love, time would fly by faster. If you begrudgingly do the work, you would build up internal resistance against it, and make yourself increasingly unhappy and exhausted.

Every day, when you wake up instead of being disappointed and depressed that you are not going to work at your dream job, be grateful that you have a job that is supporting you, as there are others who would love to have it. This perspective will invigorate you to do your work with love, and smile while you are at it. You would find that instead of feeling drained at the end of the day, you have energy left to look for your dream job after work.

If you do not find your dream job, at least you know that you are giving the best of yourself. That is rewarding in itself, and somebody of influence may recognize how good you are at what you do where you are, and the attitude with which you do it, and present you with a better opportunity to promote you either in your current workplace or elsewhere.

Be fair to yourself by doing your work with love, whether or not you love the work or love working there. It will bring out the best in you that will make you stand out to others, and could finally lead you to a job that you love, and love doing. Life rewards justly in due course.

104.

Pray a New Kind of Prayer

Many people need a friend or an authority who brings them hope, uplifts them, and one in whom they can trust completely, especially during tumultuous times. This need leads them to turn to God in prayer. People, however, tend to pray from a begging, fault-finding, and complaining position. God, please give me this, give me that; I need, I need, I need. God, why do bad things happen to me? God, why don't those people change? When you pray like this your world will remain dark, and you will not experience change.

I now encourage you to start praying differently to start feeling exuberant about life. Try praying a new kind of prayer; one that is grateful, hopeful, healing, transforms, and inspires solutions. Start your prayer by being thankful to God for being alive right now and for His presence in your life. Instead of praying like a beggar, bring your petition to God as a believer, based on the foundation of unwavering faith. Turn to Him without complaining but present your requests with thanksgiving. Declare and believe that it is done and His peace will fill your heart as it goes beyond human understanding.

Praise Him and give thanks for the many blessings in your life and for what you are about to receive. Say, "Thank you God for all that you have blessed me with and for the change you are bringing, which will arrive in your perfect time and in your way. I trust in You." Say out loud what it is you are grateful about, as there is power in your words that keep you encouraged.

Thank God for providing you with solutions, direction, and the wisdom to implement, instead of complaining about what you do not like and do not have. Thank God for your money. As it leaves you instead of cursing it bless it, so it blesses other people's lives and returns to you multiplied to allow you to help yourself and others. This type of prayer shifts your thinking and feelings in a positive direction, which opens the door to allow in all that is good and bountiful.

Thank God for your health, family, friends, enemies, and workplace, as He is using these to transform you into a wiser and stronger person. Start blessing them and being grateful for them, and your perspective will change. Thank God for the car you drive. If you don't have one but use public transit, thank God for it. If you do not have this but have to walk, thank God for your feet as there are people who cannot use their feet but must rely on a wheelchair or someone to carry them, and some even drag on the ground. Thank God when something does not work out as you know He has something better planned for you.

Since I was a child, I learned the power of prayer and have used it faithfully, and especially so as an adult. It gives hope when hope is gone. It offers strength when there is none. It brings love when anger comes. It bestows understanding when differences appear. It gives clarity in the midst of clouds. It brings peace when the war is on the inside. It shows how to help when all we have is want. It offers joy when misery arrives. It heals when the pain is too much. It brings miracles out of mistakes. It gives courage when the battle is on. It comforts to let you feel as though you are never alone. It guides to show another way. It humbles to make you let go. It allows you to trust in an unseen power to take care of something that seems bigger than yourself. It makes you feel like the burden is lifted and gone.

Prayers can do all these things and much more if you learn to pray differently. I want to inspire and challenge you to start praying positively and gratefully and see what magic it works in your life. Prayer with love and faith transforms, heals, stirs, moves, and restores miraculously, for this is the power of the Creator's works. Pray a new kind of prayer to create an uplifting shift in you.

105.

Develop Faith

This ever-changing world in which we live is filled with increasing uncertainties, instability and insecurities now more than ever. And with everybody being so busy with little time to care for and help one another, faith is needed to help carry you through life.

I do not think you can find a single person in the world who can come forward, and say that everything worked out exactly how they wanted it. Everybody will experience trials and tribulations to test your substance. I am no different but what allowed me to weather the many storms of life, is my belief and faith in God as well as the support I receive from my family and friends due to their faith in God.

Scriptures say that as the body without the spirit is dead, faith without works is dead also. I extend this saying to include, "works without faith is also dead." The reason being is because you can make every effort and execute a well-developed plan to achieving something that you want, and yet there is no guarantee you would get the exact results you want, when and how you want it. But when you take action with faith in God, you know that what comes your way is what He wants for you at that moment. Your faith and trust in His divine will are what will help you to stay calm yet strong and stable through the turbulent waters.

When you do not have faith in God especially during your challenges, you leave yourself open and susceptible to suffering from depression and anxiety. In such emotional anguish, you will not be able to sail through the rough seas of life victoriously, as you feel you are drowning. As such, work with faith even when you are afraid because that is when you need to have deep-rooted trust in the Creator. Faith expands you and keeps you open to all of God's wondrous possibilities instead of being limited and restricted to the minimal scope of your desires.

When you do not get what you want, it could be because God has something bigger or better planned for you, but you need to develop faith in Him, without which you would not recognize His grace and possibilities. When you are going through your tough times, take caution, and avoid those who have no faith because they will pull you down.

One of my favorite scriptural verses that keeps my faith strong is Proverbs 3:5-6, "Trust in the Lord with all thine heart, and lean not unto thine own understanding. In all thy ways acknowledge Him, and He shall direct thy paths." This verse makes me feel supported, and I hope it does for you, too.

106.

Become Consciously Aware

Most people are operating and living at an unconscious level of existence, unaware of what is behind their suffering and most importantly what, if anything, they can do about it. To bring about effective change, you must be prepared to face the person in the mirror. Only then you are ready to become consciously aware, which requires you to deliberately and intentionally pay close attention to your life and state of being; to become alert to it. It is from here that you can face the conflicts in yourself to go beyond suffering.

To look within is a difficult task because it means you cannot look outward at others; only at yourself. It can be scary because there is nobody to point your finger at as you release a hold on your crutch; those people and things that you can blame. You are left open to now become alert to your thoughts, feelings, emotions, reactions, attitudes, behaviors, choices, outcomes, ideas and concepts that you made your own.

When you can face these boldly, then you can see how they have been working for or against you, and what you can do about them. It requires you to be present as an observer whereby there is an intense noticing, without which there is no real seeing. Only then can you make a powerful change.

Awareness is what reveals the barriers within you, such as the prejudices, fears, judgments, false limitations, conditioning, and selfishness that prevent you from enjoying and living life fully. Conscious awareness is taking action to affect change when you become aware.

Every day, take some alone time to practice becoming the objective observer of yourself, to have victory over self. Apply conscious awareness to all areas and situations in your life, as it is the only place from which illuminative change could occur.

107.

Ask This One Question

You have been on a long journey of understanding to help you gracefully maneuver your way through what often seems like the insanity of life. You have finally arrived at this destination point equipped to now ask yourself one big question. It requires you to ask no other but this one question, to be able to explore it fully.

I invite you to find a quiet space where you are physically alone in an environment conducive to relaxation; where you can sit comfortably without any noise and interruptions for a few minutes. Turn off all electronic devices including your phone. Now close your eyes and be still. Ask yourself this one question, "Who Am I?" Now extend the question with your eyes closed by asking, "Who am I without a body; without my thoughts, feelings, emotions, ideas, concepts, memories, time, perceptions and labels?" "Who am I without being this or that?" "What am I?"

When you ask your questions, do so without identification with thoughts that may arise. Do not get involved in them. Watch thought come and go. Then ask, "Who is watching thought or what is watching thought?" When you can start watching thought, a quiet will eventually take place within. You will realize that the one who is observing is neither male nor female. You are none of your roles. You are neither this nor that. You simply are; I AM. In that there is peace. Without identification with thoughts, feelings, and emotions, memories and time, perceptions and labels all that is left is emptiness yet fullness. Empty of all your ideas, concepts, concerns and labels but full of inner quiet and peace.

From this state, calmly go about your day as you are full, and everything you do will happen from a different place, one of deeper awareness; of peace. I encourage you to do this simple practice every day as soon as you awaken from sleep. Do it, even while you are commuting on the bus, train, or while walking and you will begin to become more and more aware of the "I AM" without the noise of labels, definitions, and the need to be important or superior to others, and you will feel the very thing for which you yearn—peace—which is the nature of the "I AM."

It is how you can begin to function peacefully and live the insights in this book more naturally. This is the next step in your evolution that will allow you to let go of your attachment to the things of the flesh to experience the gifts of the spirit. Keep asking your question and never give up until you experience the answer.

Acknowledgments

I convey my heartfelt appreciation to everyone who came together to make this project a reality. Thank you to all my cheerleaders for your enthusiasm and support. A special thanks to my brother, Barry Rajpaul for your warm heart and priceless creation of the beautiful image design used inside this book; my childhood friend, Ingrid Mohammed for adding some fun to this project as we explored "Willy and Wouldy;" Dana and Tammy Sirois for your immense encouragement and feedback; Ron Sanchez for our meaningful communication; and Geoffrey McCadden for your kind guidance.

Thank you to my publisher and your team for helping me realize my vision. My gratitude goes out to God, every family member, friend, business, sponsor, and anyone else who is helping to get people to read this book. It means that lives are being reshaped and lifted to a new level.

Finally, I would like to thank all my readers in advance for your feedback, and for taking the time to read these insights, as I know your life will be deeply touched and transformed in the end. You help make my writing and sharing fulfilling.

Thank you!

Printed in Great Britain
by Amazon

36254894R00142